LEAN CHANGE MANAGEMENT

INNOVATIVE PRACTICES FOR MANAGING ORGANIZATIONAL CHANGE

JASON LITTLE

HMEXPRESS

TABLE OF CONTENTS

I
INTRODUCTION

A STORY HOW
IT ALL BEGUN

I. INTRODUCTION

When the shoving started, I thought to myself, "What the hell have I gotten myself into?"

Certain moments in your life are unforgettable, and I will never forget my experience at the AYE (Amplify Your Effectiveness) conference, where I learned why change is so difficult.

Until that time, my experience as a change agent was limited to helping organizations adopt Agile software practices. The Agile movement started with the creation of the Agile Manifesto in 2001. At its core, it's a set of four values and twelve principles that spawned a variety of processes, methods, and practices.

I had focused on learning these processes, methods, and practices and lulled myself into a false sense of security that I knew it all. At its core, none of this stuff was *rocket surgery*; it was simply a set of common-sense practices for building better software. How could anyone *not* get it?

Shows how little I knew.

I remember walking into Steve Smith's session on change having no idea what to expect. Steve was one of the five AYE Conference hosts. Now, this was a big step for me. I knew a couple of people at this conference but, as the typical introvert who scans the room to latch onto a friendly face, I found only unfamiliar ones. Forty of us formed a circle of chairs, and Steve asked us to answer the question, "How do you feel about change?" I was sitting two chairs away from Steve and hoped the order of answers would be random — but no such luck!

Before I could think, or even reword the answers of the people before me, I heard these words fall out of my mouth: *"I like change! Change is exciting, fresh, and new, and I think shake-ups are needed every now and then!"*

Phew, I passed that hurdle with no major problems.

Once everyone had the opportunity to answer that question, Steve started a simulation designed to have people experience the *Virginia Satir Change Model* [1]. This five-stage change model describes the effects each stage of a change has on feelings, thoughts, performance, and physiology.

The stages of the Satir Change Model:

- *Stage 1 – Late Status Quo:*
  Everything is familiar and comfortable, and performance is stable.

- *Stage 2 – Foreign Element:*
  This stage is about resistance. In my view, Agile is a powerful Foreign Element that generates a strong response from people. Some love it, others resist it.

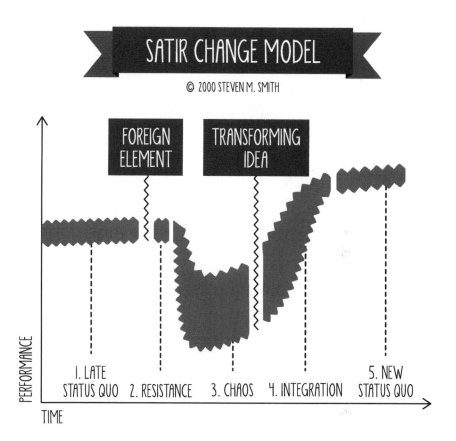

Virginia Satir Change Model by Steven M. Smith.

- *Stage 3 – Chaos:*
  People feel that they're losing their identity and experience a
  general sense of loss, which leads to a drop in productivity and
  an increase in confusion or anger.

- *Stage 4 – The Transforming Idea, Practice and Integration:*
  Once people have tumbled through *Chaos*, they reach the
  point where they *get it*. They hit *The Transforming Idea. The
  Transforming Idea* leads into *Practice and Integration.* Here,

people integrate the benefits of the *Foreign Element* into their new identity.

- *Stage 5 – New Status Quo:*
  Performance starts to stabilize at a higher level than it was during the *Late Status Quo*.

Back to the conference session...

One person was elected to be the *Star* of the session, and the other participants were divided into groups that represented different stages of the Satir Change Model. Each person had a different task.

- I was part of the *Late Status Quo* group, which was responsible for keeping the *Star* in one corner of the room.

- The *New Status Quo* group was responsible for moving the *Star* to the opposite corner of the room.

- The *Foreign Element* group was responsible for triggering the change.

- *Chaos* was responsible for disrupting the process.

I remember Steve saying, *"I don't know what's going to happen here, but let's start!"* Then, the simulation started, and my group did what any rational group would have done.

We built a wall. Literally.

Really. We looted the hotel for tables, chairs, plants, and anything else we could find to build a physical wall that would keep the *New Status Quo* out and the *Star* in. We also borrowed the fancy chairs in the lobby to set up a cozy place within our compound to keep the *Star* comfortable! I will never forget the looks directed our way from the hotel staff.

The *Foreign Element* group ended up doing most of *Chaos'* job, and they gave a performance worthy of an Academy Award! They chanted, sang and banged on garbage cans. As they were disrupting, the *New Status Quo* group decided that it was time to take down the wall so they could get at the *Star*.

They started pulling the tables and chairs down, and we put them back up.

Then they took them down again.

And we put them back up.

Soon after, a shoving match started, and Steve had to step in. If you've never met Steve, he is about 6-foot-3 and has a booming voice, so when he put his hands in the air and yelled, *"Hold it!"*...we stopped.

After the room of highly enlightened coaches and agents of change realized what they had done and calmed down, Steve restarted the simulation.

The *New Status Quo* somehow learned that the *Star* was a huge fan of Johanna Rothman, who was facilitating a session in the room beside us. They asked Johanna to come over, and that's all it took for the *Star* to vacate the *Late Status Quo* compound and relocate to the *New Status Quo* area.

TRY AS YOU MAY, CHANGE CANNOT BE CONTROLLED

PEOPLE HAVE A WAY OF FIGHTING THROUGH THE PAIN OF CHANGE WHEN THEY WANT THE OUTCOME BADLY ENOUGH

To this day I still have *"Aha!"* moments about what happened that day. I wrote about the experience in my blog that same day, and indicated that the message was received loud and clear: Try as you may, change cannot be controlled. Oddly enough, my brain hears that message in Steve's booming voice!

As I wrestled with this opening chapter, I had another *"Aha!"* moment. The *New Status Quo* created the ultimate motivator for the *Star* when they brought in Johanna. It didn't matter how chaotic the room was, or what obstacles were in the way; the *Star* was motivated to talk to Johanna, and he didn't stop until he made it to the other corner of the room.

This leads me to answer the question, *"Why did you write this book?"*

I wrote this book for people who are passionate about bringing meaningful change into their organizations. I want to help them broaden their toolkit by filling it with ideas from Agile, Lean Startup, neuroscience, psychology, organizational development and change management. Of course, while this book will help you stock up your toolkit with tools; *you'll* have to decide which tool to pull and when to pull it!

Many of the stories in this book are about my experiences with triggering change through the introduction of Agile software practices, but at the end of the day, change is change. And this is not just my conclusion: many people I talked to while writing this book confirm that these ideas can be applied to any organizational change.

Organizational change is a powerful *Foreign Element* that brings uncertainty and provokes an emotional response from people. The product development world has learned to manage uncertainty better with Lean Startup. I will get you up to speed about Lean Startup later on. For now, I'll tell you that its principles can be applied to change by involving those affected by the change in the design of the change. That involvement will validate that it is the change that is most likely to work, and it will likely reduce the symptom of *change resistance.*

Yes, I refer to *resistance* as a symptom.

The annual *Version One State of Agile Development* survey cites that change resistance is one cause for Agile failure. There are many studies from the change management world that reach similar conclusions. A study from Onirik [2] cites two reasons why change initiatives fail. The first is the unpredictable nature of those pesky humans, and the second is the lack of a structured change process.

Taking ideas from the *Satir Change Model* and other psychology models, change agents can understand that different people process change at different rates and different intensities. Someone who values certainty, and is highly averse to risk, may appear resistant until they understand the benefits of the change – or if the change interferes with their belief system. Change agents need to know how to help them understand the benefits the *Foreign Element* brings. Sometimes, this means involving them in the design a new process in order to motivate them.

As for the notion that we should "check our emotions at the door" when we come to work? Not going to happen – and that's a good thing. People are emotional creatures, and that emotional response is a sign that change is happening. This is why change agents need to understand how the brain reacts to change and how to focus on ability and motivation to help bring successful change into organizations.

Finally, taking ideas from traditional organizational development and change management can help change agents manage the uncertainty, resistance and emotional response to change.

I believe combining ideas from different communities can help change agents better understand change dynamics, which will move the slider further away from plan-driven approaches, and towards feedback-driven approaches.

Remember, your change doesn't begin on the start-date written on your Gantt chart. It begins when people are whispering at the water-cooler, *"Did you hear they're doing a re-org? Am I fired?"* If you rely solely on plans, you're planning to fail.

This book will help you navigate the murky and messy waters of change. It will stock up your toolkit with tools, but you'll have to decide which tool to pull, and when to pull it!

Finally, this book is not a recipe that you'll follow to *ensure successful change*. This book will help you become a chef, if you're willing to put in the time and effort. Sometimes, your Crème Brûlée will come out nicely toasted, sometimes you'll burn it beyond recognition – either way, you will be on the path to knowing how to facilitate meaningful change that improves people's lives.

2
THE COMMISSION

APPLYING LEAN STARTUP TO CHANGE

2. THE COMMISSION

"James isn't motivated. I gave him a book to learn about HTML, and he didn't even bother to read it!"

Puzzled, I asked my friend, who was also James' manager, if she had set the expectation that the job would require technical skills when James was hired. *"Well, no,"* she replied, *"but we need somebody who isn't just a project manager. They have to be able to jump in and help with anything."*

I went to my desk and grabbed a copy of *Behind Closed Doors* [1], a fantastic book about management from Esther Derby and Johanna Rothman. (I highly recommend reading it, but after you've read the rest of *my* book of course!)

In a friendly, uplifting tone, I said, *"You know Sheila, **you** really should read this book; it's about how to be a great manager!"* And I handed it to her.

"Oh crap…" was all she could mutter.

At that moment, Sheila realized her well-intentioned gesture probably upset James. After all, from her perspective, this was a simple change. All he had to do was read a book, so why didn't he just do it? Sheila was under pressure to get client work done, but from James' perspective, he was simply being told to read a book. He had no idea how that helped Sheila or the project.

Sheila and James had different perspectives on the situation. Perspective matters. It's human nature to label someone as being resistant to change when they don't do what we want them to. As a Change Agent, it's never about you, or me – it's about understanding the perspective of the people affected by change. People may be afraid of the loss that comes with change, but may also just not understand the reason behind the change.

LEAN CHANGE MANAGEMENT MOVES THE SLIDER FOR MANAGING CHANGE FROM USING PLAN-DRIVEN APPROACHES TO FEEDBACK-DRIVEN APPROACHES

Change brings disruption, and if you remember the story from Chapter 1, what started as a simulation about change turned into a World Wrestling Entertainment-style change agent Battle Royale! You may think the change you want to implement is trivial, but it can have a tremendous effect on the person being asked to change.

The main story weaved throughout this book focuses on a real organization that I'll refer to as The Commission. The names and dates have been changed to protect the innocent, or guilty, depending on *your* perspective! ☺

From my perspective, The Commission was an organization I assumed would be extremely difficult to change. It was a large and slow moving public sector organization, where people had worked for decades, and had seen every management fad come and go. Mix all that together, and I assumed the effort to change The Commission would be akin to pushing water uphill with a stick.

Let me be clear: this is not a slight against The Commission. In today's digital age, all organizations are challenged with keeping up with the torrid pace of change. I simply assumed breaking the status quo was going to be really hard.

In retrospect, I think the approach to change being introduced at The Commission was the *spaghetti on the wall* approach. That is, throw a bunch of changes at the wall, and hope some of them stick. Many large changes were already in flight before I started:

- Infrastructure had recently been outsourced and the transition to the new outsourced organization had started

- One hundred people had been laid off, although since many were unionized employees, they would still be working for 6 months

- A multi-year modernization program to migrate off legacy systems, and onto a new application platform was starting

These changes sound simple enough when they are listed as bullet points, however, in reality, these three changes affected thousands of people. To further complicate the matter, senior management wanted to toss another big change on the pile: the Kanban transformation. The Commission was going to be migrating their software development practices to Lean and Agile methods, which they called "the Kanban transformation."

As if these four massive changes weren't enough to shake up the place, one-third of the staff would be retiring within the next few years, and the functional silos were made out of steel. Simply put, the number of changes going on at the same time was high.

The new CIO had hired a consulting firm he worked with in the past to kick off the Kanban transformation. Next he created a Quality Management Office (QMO) that would be composed of internal employees. The QMO would be taking over the responsibility of managing the Kanban transformation from the consultants when their contract was up.

I wasn't fond of the QMO label, but I was excited to join the team. I knew some of the consultants, and I heard they were using Lean Startup principles to execute the Kanban transformation project. I had recently left an organization where I launched two new products using the Lean Startup method, and also won a Lean Startup competition, so I was curious to see how they would apply this approach to change.

Before I continue, let me briefly explain what Lean Startup is. If you are already familiar with the Lean Startup, go ahead and skip the explanation below.

WHAT IS LEAN STARTUP?

In the old days, companies would spend vast amounts of money developing products nobody wanted, and then spend some more trying to convince customers that they really, really had the problem their new product solved.

The *"build it, and they will come....hopefully..."* approach to product development was getting more difficult.

Prior to joining The Commission, I worked for a company that had tried this approach. It took them over a year and US$1.5 million to develop a new product, which they eventually killed off because no one bought it. That's right, not a single sale. The CEO didn't want to experience that pain again, so I used the Lean Startup Method to bring two new products to market. Within three months, they generated US$160,000 of opportunities and US$39,000 of revenue. The total cost of bringing these two products to market was three months of my salary. The products paid for themselves pretty quickly.

The Lean Startup Method teaches organizations how to develop their market and build demand for their new product before they spend all their cash building something no one will buy. Lean Startup organizations do this through a looping **Build, Measure, and Learn** cycle.

1. Build a Minimum Viable Product (MVP), which is designed to test your assumptions about how customers will respond to your product. If you think potential customers will use five features of your new product, your MVP could simply be releasing one of those features you think is the most valuable.

2. Measure the response to your MVP through, what Lean Startup calls, "pirate metrics":
    - Acquisition: Get a new customer
    - Activation: The new customer signs-up and use the product
    - Retention: The customer comes back and uses it again
    - Referral: The customer shares the product with their friends
    - Revenue: The customer pays for your product

3. Learn about how people use the product from your measurements, and feed that data into your next MVP.

PROCESS HELPS MAKE SENSE OF CHANGE BUT BLINDLY FOLLOWING A PROCESS IS A RECIPE FOR DISASTER

And repeat. Another way to think of Lean Startup is that it's like Dr. Deming's PDCA (Plan Do Check Act) loop, only cooler. Oh, and during the beta reader phase of writing this book a friend and colleague, Geoff Schadt, pointed out that Deming actually got the PDCA idea from his mentor, Shewart [2]. Thanks Geoff!

And now, back to the story.

The consultants at The Commission were applying these ideas by running change initiatives they called Minimum Viable Changes, or MVCs. This relabelling of Lean Startup's MVP puzzled me because *minimal* doesn't always mean *small*. As I mentioned in Chapter 1, even the smallest change can be massively disruptive to the person affected – I prefer to call change initiatives *Experiments* instead. After all, how people will respond to change is difficult to predict.

The approach the consultants took to applying Lean Startup principles to change was for each change agent to create an MVC. Each MVC had a hypothesis and one or more measurements. Once introduced, we'd monitor the progress towards the outcome we predicted through our hypothesis.

Here's an example:

The Commission's Architecture team wanted to learn more about Lean and Agile practices. My hypothesis stated that by visualizing their work on a Kanban board and introducing a daily standup meeting, they would be able to more effectively co-ordinate their work as a team. The measurements were things like how often they did stand-ups, and how they worked as a team despite being "officially assigned" to certain projects.

The minimal aspect of the MVC, meant that I was only introducing basic practices that would require minimal disruption to their normal routine.

We would review the outcome of the MVC's bi-weekly, and then we would decide to Pursue, Pivot, or Abandon the change.

- **Pursue** meant that the change worked, and we should keep doing similar changes. For example, if the MVC was to introduce a technical Agile practice with the team, and they ran with it, we'd do more of those instead of strictly Agile process techniques.

- **Pivot** meant that the change sorta worked, but something about it required tweaking. For example, if the MVC was to introduce an automated testing tool and the team liked the idea of automating tests, but found the tool hard to use, we'd pick another one.

- **Abandon** meant...well, forget about it, it's probably not the right time for the change. Yet.

The Architecture team's MVC was a simple change involving a mature team, so I'll give you another example. To do that, I will need to pick on everyone's favorite software project artifact – the Status Report. Status reports tend to be reported as green until a few weeks before the end date. Then suddenly all the risks pile up, and the status indicator turns red. Executives often question the validity of the green status report, but also complain if they see a red status report too early. This problem isn't unique to The Commission!

To counter-balance this problem, my colleague and friend, Andrew Annett had an idea to start all projects red [3]! His thought was that at the beginning of the project you have a pocket full of money and an empty head, with respect to project knowledge, so you need to learn your way to the prestigious green status.

The red/green status idea had to be evaluated, so we came up with an Experiment. The Experiment – remember I'm referring to MVC's as Experiments – was to float the idea with a few key people and see whether or not their eyes would pop out of their heads. This is a great example of why the MVC term bugged me. I'd call messing with the beloved Status Report a maximum non-viable change!

No eyeballs were harmed during the introduction of this Experiment, but the violent reaction, metaphorically speaking, was enough for us to toss it into the *Abandon all hope* bucket.

After I had been on the team for a couple of weeks, we had our regular retrospective meeting. One of the consultants asked me to say something fluffy because I was the *fluffy Agile guy*. After thinking for a minute, I said, *"Well, it seems we're using the Lean Startup lingo, but not really using any Lean Startup principles. Our changes are prescriptive; we decide whether or not they work, and we change them every two weeks. It's pissing people off and personally, I'm burned out."*

Others seemed to share that feeling, but it took me and my big mouth to say it out loud! That seemed to kick start something, although that's my perspective, which – as you know – is objective and not biased at all! ☺

Over time, our approach in the QMO changed radically, and we began pulling ideas and models from other areas of knowledge and communities that would help us facilitate organizational change. You'll learn about many of those ideas and models in this book.

LEAN CHANGE MANAGEMENT IS ABOUT FUNDAMENTALLY CHANGING HOW WE THINK ABOUT CHANGE

The book you have in your hands (or on your digital device) was inspired by Jurgen Appelo's Mojito Method. That is, combining ideas and models from many communities creates a model that is more effective than each of the individual ideas themselves.

The massive changes The Commission was undertaking had an enormous emotional effect on more than 3000 people, but it needed to be done. The Commission was nearing its organizational shelf-life, they were using decades old systems, and the people who knew how to run them were closing in on retirement. Trying to change that while simultaneously changing how they managed work and people was a daunting task to say the least. Facilitating transformational change such as this is hard, and today's plan-driven approaches to change are not equipped to manage this degree of complexity.

As complexity increases, so does uncertainty.

In the next chapter, I'll describe what the Lean Change Management cycle is and how we used it to navigate this complexity. Sometimes our experiments worked as planned, and sometimes they failed miserably.

3

LEAN CHANGE MANAGEMENT CYCLE

A FEEDBACK-DRIVEN MODEL
FOR MANAGING CHANGE

3. LEAN CHANGE MANAGEMENT CYCLE

"All models are wrong, but some are useful" is a phrase credited to George Box [1]. George Box was a Professor of Statistics at the University of Wisconsin, and a pioneer in the world of quality control. What I believe he meant was that simple models can be useful for making sense of complex situations, even if they are not 100% correct, 100% of the time.

I struggled with how to refer to Lean Change Management in the first edition of this book back in September 2012. Should it be called a model? A framework? A process? A method?

In the end, I decided that I'm not concerned with the label. You'll form your own opinion, so for now, let's stick with calling Lean Change Management a model.

Here's a brief explanation of the Lean Change Management cycle:

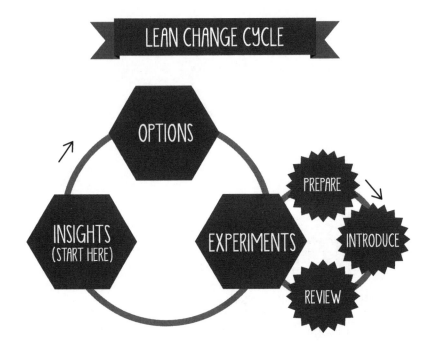

A non-linear, feedback-driven model for managing change.

- **Insights**: Before you can plan any change, you need to understand the current state of the organization. To do that, there are many tools, assessments, and models you can apply to understand the current state. For example, at The Commission, we collected Insights by using an ADKAR® assessment and informal meetings called Lean Coffee. You'll learn more about those in Chapters 4 and 5.

- **Options**: Once you've gained enough Insights to start planning, you need Options. Options have a cost, value and impact. Options usually include one or more hypotheses and expected benefits. These hypotheses are turned into Experiments when you are ready to introduce a change.

- **Experiments**: At this point you've learned enough about your current state and considered multiple Options. Now it's time to introduce a change and see if it works out the way you thought it would.

Experiments also have a sub-cycle:

- **Prepare**: This is the planning stage of your Experiment. Later on in this book I describe some light-weight planning and sense-making tools you can use to prepare your Experiments. The key point about the Prepare step is that at this point, all you have are your assumptions about the change. It is in this step that you validate your approach with the people affected by the change *before* you implement it.

- **Introduce**: This is the step where you start working with the people affected by the change. Once a change has reached this step, it's considered to be in process. Ideally you will be limiting the number of changes happening at the same time.

- **Review**: Here you review the outcomes of the Experiment. Typically you do this after the amount of time you thought would be needed for the change to stick.

Let's look at some examples of how we used this cycle at The Commission.

GAINING INSIGHTS

In addition to the consultants and the QMO, The Commission had an official Change Management department that helped manage all the changes that were happening. They were using the assessment tool called the ADKAR® Method [2].

UNDERSTAND THE DYNAMICS OF YOUR ORGANIZATION BY COLLECTING INSIGHTS WITH A VARIETY OF TOOLS FROM DIFFERENT COMMUNITIES

ADKAR® is a perfect example of why I refer to Lean Change Management as a model and **not** a process or method. Here's why:

The assessment portion of the ADKAR® method was an Experiment that had an output that fed into our Insights. Did you notice how I just changed the order of the steps of the Lean Change Management cycle? We started with an Experiment (an actual change) that would generate Insights (that would help us define future changes).

All change management processes start with some type of assessment before the change project starts. Some call that approach *understanding change readiness*. When we sent out the survey for the ADKAR® assessment, the change process started, whether we liked it or not!

Before I continue, let me give you a brief explanation of what ADKAR® is.

ADKAR® is a method created by Prosci. They research organizational change, and believe that change is a cumulative product of the personal change journeys of each individual within the organization.

Their most famous tool – ADKAR®, describes five conditions that must be satisfied in order for that individual change journey to progress. Organizational change happens when people progress through those five conditions.

1. **Awareness** of the need for change
2. **Desire** to participate in and support the change
3. **Knowledge** on how to change
4. **Ability** to implement required skills and behaviors
5. **Reinforcement** to sustain the change

These five conditions fall into the natural order of how an individual experiences the change. For example, if you have no *Awareness* that your organization is adopting Agile practices, you cannot have the *Desire* to implement it.

Here's a personal example:

I know the way I do accounting for my business is slow and error-prone. I know how to fix the problem (Knowledge in ADKAR®), but I simply have no desire to do so. It's easier for me to use the software and process I have in place now, instead of learning a new tool and going through the anguish of migrating all my historical data. I have more important things to worry about, like writing the rest of this book!

According to Prosci, if any of these five conditions are weak, the change will stall and fail.

At The Commission, the ADKAR® assessment results showed us that the *Desire* with staff was high. The lowest scores were in the *Knowledge* and *Ability* areas which gave us hints about how to approach some of the changes.

Regardless of how you kick off your change project, people are already talking about it, so you are *starting* in the middle of a constantly changing reality. This is why I say that your change process begins the very moment you send out anything about it, like the ADKAR®

DECIDE ON OPTIONS BASED ON WHAT YOU LEARNED FROM COLLECTING INSIGHTS

assessment that was sent out at The Commission.

WHAT ARE OUR OPTIONS?

Back at The Commission, after collecting Insights about how people felt about the change, we needed to create Options. Some were obvious, such as training and team coaching. People were eventually going to need to learn what these new practices were.

Other Options weren't so obvious, but were definitely necessary. I realized we needed to increase communication, so an Option I created was to use Lean Coffee. Lean Coffee [3] is an informal, yet structured approach for managing meetings and discussions that I'll explain in greater detail in Chapter 4. I thought the Lean Coffee sessions would help me connect with people from different areas of the organization so I could start establishing relationships. (Always a useful thing when implementing change.)

Regardless of which Options we came up with, the tricky part was understanding all that would be necessary to make the Options viable! For example, helping people acquire knowledge through training is one thing, but changing behavior and having them apply what they learned, is a completely different challenge.

Another Option I considered was creating a blog or newsletter to push out more information about the Kanban transformation. Sure, we were already going to do formal coaching and training, but increasing

Kanban transformation awareness and transparency would help too. Each of these Options had a cost, value, and impact associated with them. At The Commission, we were prioritizing our Options by cost and value on a chart, and then we'd have a quick discussion about the impact.

As a reminder, the cost of any Option is not necessarily about the cold hard cash. A high-cost Option can be one that requires more effort, like creating a blog or newsletter where you need to allocate a significant amount of time to brainstorming, research, and writing. (Much like writing a book, come to think of it!) In this case, we'd need more thought, effort, and help from other areas of the organization, which equals a higher cost for that Option.

Lean Coffee, on the other hand, is a low-cost Option. I could host it myself (no long approval process) and hold the entire meeting quickly, which in turn allowed me to evaluate the results of that Experiment faster and adjust my next steps.

The value of an Option is the payoff I expect to gain based on my assumptions. Think of the payoff as the return on investment (ROI) of the Option. Sometimes your payoff is based on gut-feel and your measurement can be as simple as asking the person affected by the change if they're happier working this way.

I may drop an Option entirely if the expected value is low and the cost is high. While that makes logical sense to *me*, I always recommend that you talk about it with your change team because chances are, someone will have good ideas on how to improve the viability of that Option.

Here's how I originally plotted my Options at The Commission:

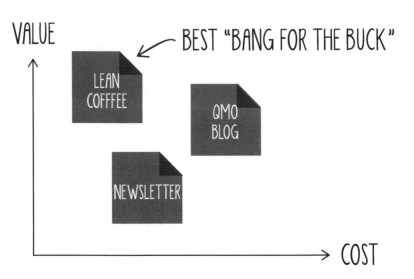

Quickly plot Options considering the cost and expected value.

Options and Benefits

- **Lean Coffee**: Low Cost, High Value. It would be simple, logistically speaking, and the payoff had high-value potential...if people showed up!

- **QMO Team Blog**: Medium-to-High Cost, Medium value. This one had great value, but a variable cost, and you'll understand why with this one word: Sharepoint (if you don't believe me, just search the internet for Sharepoint...on second thought: better not! Just trust me. ☺)

- **Newsletter**: Low Cost, Medium Value. While the newsletter had a low cost, it was a bit higher than Lean Coffee, and it might seem pushy and impersonal by comparison.

Working with Options is as much art as it is science. There is no formula or best practice to follow. Remember, the Options you create are from your point of view. You will need to consider how disruptive that Option might be for other people and for the organization.

TIME FOR EXPERIMENTS!

The final step in the Lean Change Management model is to create an Experiment based on the selected Option. At this point, all members of the change team were creating hypotheses and measurements with our Minimum Viable Changes (MVCs). I wasn't sure how to form a hypothesis about the Lean Coffee Experiment, but I did know what I wanted to learn: I wanted to see who would show up, which departments they were from, and what topics they wanted to discuss.

I thought the Lean Coffee sessions would provide me with the Insights that would help me think of new Options.

WHAT I LEARNED

Fifteen people showed up at the first Lean Coffee session. This was a pleasant surprise because I had only posted signs about this session throughout the building; no formal invite was sent out by email. Earlier I described how the newsletter was low-cost, but could be seen as pushy, since I'd be shoving content into someone's inbox rather than give them the option to show up for a Lean Coffee session.

Most of the attendees were business analysts, but one person who worked in the Project Management Office (PMO) showed up. He had a background in Lean, so when he saw the "Lean" Coffee sign he decided to check it out.

This sign was posted in high foot-traffic areas in the building.

A person from the PMO! I was pumped! Getting connected to the PMO in the context of moving to Agile practices is the holy grail of Agile change! I showed him how we were using Kanban within the IT department, and he then connected me with the rest of the PMO team. Later on, the PMO would become one of the strongest supporters of the Agile practices we were trying to introduce at The Commission.

Over the next few months, attendance at the Lean Coffee sessions faded, as the novelty-factor wore off, but the core attendees kept coming back week after week. This simple Experiment helped us figure out who the early adopters were. This is perhaps one of the most important aspects of bringing change, any change, into an organization. Find the people that are motivated to learn, and help them become change agents. Once other employees see their colleagues are motivated to support the change, it will help reduce resistance to change. The people who kept returning to the Lean Coffee sessions were business analysts, and eventually a business analysis Community of Practice (CoP) was started. The Lean Coffee

Experiment had such a positive impact that soon a new and similar Experiment emerged – Executive Lean Coffee!

Executive Lean Coffee sessions created the opportunity for employees to talk directly to the executives, but it didn't last long. The reality of the modernization program was starting to creep in, and the urgent work became a higher priority.

A LOOP ISN'T LINEAR

As a change agent, I'm perpetually looking for Insights. At The Commission, we collected Insights from interviews, water cooler conversations, official surveys, and more. Sometimes we had a flood of data to analyze, but by using the Insights, Options, and Experiment model loop, we were able to make sense of the day-to-day change chaos.

Sometimes my only Insight was *"Um, I'm not sure what to do about this problem"*. In that case, I'd try an Experiment. There is no specific order to follow; you simply need to decide how to use the model in your context.

While the stories I used to explain the Insights, Options, and Experiments model loop are simple, they do explain how to deal with the constantly developing reality change agents are faced with every day.

How do you manage a big organizational change with such a lightweight model? The easy answer is, think small!

The more in-depth answer will unfold in the next chapters. I'll show you how we borrowed ideas from different communities to help us navigate through the murky waters of change at The Commission.

4
INSIGHTS

UNDERSTAND WHAT MAKES YOUR ORGANIZATION TICK

4. INSIGHTS

"Are there any land mines I should avoid if I go talk to the PMO about the changes we're implementing in IT? They'll probably be affected at some point too."

I asked the director that the QMO team, my team, reported to. Usually I'd disrupt the place and ask for forgiveness later, but I thought it would be nice to try something different!

"No problem, go for it!" she replied.

Most organizations I've worked with had strong processes created by a PMO, and those processes were usually **really** hard to change. Worse, those processes are typically at odds with how Agile portfolios and projects are managed. It was refreshing to validate that I wasn't walking into a field of land mines.

The QMO, worked closely with the PMO throughout the Kanban transformation, but we never tried to change *them*. Our stance was to help them understand what was different about how projects were governed with the new Agile practices so *they* could decide what to change.

Remember, the Commission was already undergoing big changes, including the PMO. They were evolving from solely focusing on strategy to looking at lower-level processes. That change in focus was confusing because they now had to move further into the details of projects than they were used to. They also had to figure out how the Lean and Agile practices we were implementing in IT would affect them. That's a lot of change at once.

As we saw in the previous chapter, Insights is the first step of the Lean Change Management model, but *change* has no logical starting point. As a change agent, you're always stepping into the middle of constantly evolving reality. Traditional, plan-driven approaches assume change has a logical starting point because the change project has a start date. The plan that gets created is based on a snapshot of organizational insights generated at a certain point in time, and from a certain point of view. By the time the plan is put in practice, the reality has changed, and the plan is no longer up to date.

Plans become obsolete so quickly because there is too much emphasis on trying to create a perfect change plan. When the stakeholders and change team spend too much time planning, they run the risk of convincing themselves that the plan is perfect. Then they hit a wall of change resistance when they put the plan into practice. Of course they do!

If it took them three months to plan the change, the stakeholders and change team will have a three-month head start understanding and processing all the details of the plan. The people affected by the change need at least as much time, if not more, to catch up. You can't expect people to process and understand the plan when you surprise them with it.

Don't get me wrong, having an overall plan is important, but breaking it down into smaller chunks, and releasing those changes to the organization slowly is more important. This approach will reduce the chaos caused by introducing too many simultaneous changes. It also gives the people affected by the change the opportunity to help shape future changes. I refer to this as a feedback-driven approach for creating change plans.

This feedback starts at the first step of the Lean Change Management model: Insights. Insights can be generated from a variety of practices and assessments, such as running Lean Coffee sessions, or doing an ADKAR® assessment. After you've gathered Insights, you create Options based on different points of view, such as considering the differences and similarities between how managers feel about the change, versus how staff feel about the change. This helps the change team eliminate their perspective biases from the plan, and incorporate perspectives from those being ultimately affected by the change.

IF YOU TRULY WANT TO UNDERSTAND SOMETHING, TRY TO CHANGE IT.
- KURT LEWIN -

Said in a different way, sometimes you don't know how to start facilitating change. You need to do *something* in order to get the feedback that will guide you to the next step. After all, it is only after you act and receive feedback, that you truly understand the impact of the changes you have in mind.

Collect insights from a variety of practices and assessments.

There are many approaches for generating Insights, and it can be confusing to figure out where to start. To make it easier, I'll break down some of the approaches the QMO used, into 2 categories:

- **Practices:** Tactical actions such as sending out surveys, having informal meetings like Lean Coffee, or using Agile retrospectives to get feedback about how the change project is going.

- **Assessments:** Traditional change management tools like the ADKAR® assessment I mentioned earlier, employee engagement measurement tools, or cultural assessment tools.

PRACTICES THAT GENERATE INSIGHTS

Practices are specific actions or processes your use to generate Insights. While many change management processes have their own practices, there's no reason why you can't combine many practices from many communities to help you generate Insights. After all, if the only tool you have is a hammer, every problem will start looking like a nail.

While there are many practices for generating Insights, I'll focus on the ones I've found the most valuable:

1. Information Radiators
2. Lean Coffee
3. Culture Hacking
4. Retrospectives
5. Force Field Analysis

Practice 1: Creating and Using Information Radiators

"Want to check out our big visible portfolio wall?" I asked after a chance meeting with Sarah, one of the senior members of the PMO. *"Sure, I'd love to!"* she replied enthusiastically.

"I see you have a column for project inception, funding, and then delivery", she said as she pulled one of the sticky notes off the wall. She handed it to me and said, *"Interesting, are you guys working on this?"*

I looked at the sticky note and replied, *"Yes, if it's in the 'delivery' column, it's being worked on."*

Puzzled, she said, *"Hmm, I manage that portfolio and I know the budget hasn't been approved for this yet."*

"Really?" I said, not at all surprised. *"You should talk to Kevin. He usually gets involved at project inception, and he'd be a better person to ask. I only manage the sticky notes!"*

Long story short, Sarah and Kevin had a conversation in front of the big visible portfolio wall, and removed the project tickets that hadn't been approved yet. Did all of those projects actually stop? Maybe, maybe not, but the point is making the work visible leads to these type of exchanges. Project teams were swamped with work and it seemed like new projects were starting daily. The interesting part of this interaction between Sarah and Kevin was they agreed that they needed to work together more to keep priorities aligned. Since Sarah was a strategic portfolio manager in the PMO, and Kevin was one of the key people involved in project inception, they certainly had the reach, and clout, to make a difference in how many projects were inflight.

INFORMATION RADIATORS HELP BUILD TRUST BY MAKING WORK TRANSPARENT

This only happened because we visualized the work and provoked a conversation in front of it with the people who could make a difference. Sometimes that level of visibility provokes uncomfortable conversations, but it's necessary in order to make positive progress.

Alistair Cockburn uses the phrase "Information Radiators" [1] to describe these kinds of displays. Other people call them "visual management tools".

The point is, they're big, easy-to-read, and help everyone understand the complexity of knowledge work. Sometimes people new to Agile project management think it's a little silly to use sticky notes on a wall to represent work, however, sticky notes can help manage any level of complexity, no matter how big your project portfolio is.

Visualizing work for a 300 person department.

At The Commission, we had created a massive information radiator, we called the Enterprise Kanban Board (EKB), that represented all the work that was in progress. The board itself was 8 feet tall and 20 feet wide, and we'd often brag about having the biggest Kanban board on the eastern seaboard! We had taken over a large photocopier room, and this room was lovingly referred to as *the Nerve Centre of the transformation* because managers and directors would meet in front of it three times a week to discuss risks, issues, and blockers.

In the Agile world, this is typical. Visualizing work on a wall using sticky notes promotes more effective collaboration and cooperation, compared to stuffing all the details into an electronic tool, like Microsoft Project.

Here's another example of an information radiator I used at a different organization. The purpose of this one was to help visualize how teams were progressing through another organizational change triggered by the adoption of Agile practices.

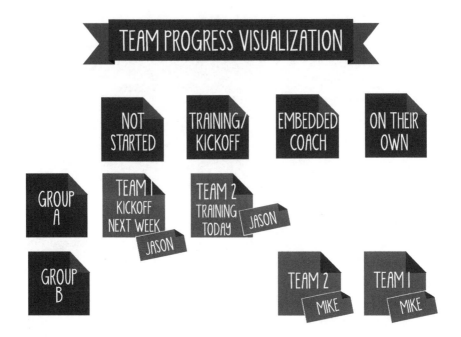

Visualizing the progress of teams adopting the change.

This organization had 600 employees, and the IT department had 13 teams and 120 people. Every morning the VP of Engineering and change team had a daily standup meeting in front of this team's board. We'd briefly talk about what obstacles the team was facing and how they were adjusting to the change.

The simple practice of visualizing progress, to me, is more effective than the emailed status reports that people want, but rarely read.

Added Bonus: The Insights Door

At The Commission, in addition to visualizing the progress of our changes, we also provided an opportunity for people to give us

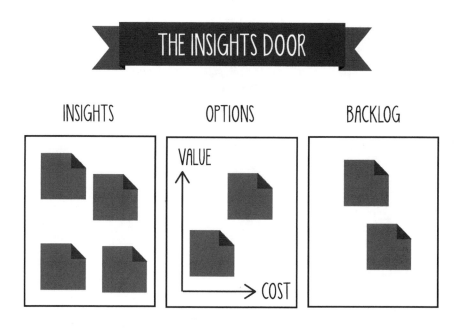

From Insights, to Options, to the backlog of changes.

anonymous feedback via what we called the Insights Door. I think you can figure out why we called it that!

We encouraged people to post sticky notes with comments when they needed help or had concerns about the changes we were implementing. Most of the time it was only the change team that used the Insights Door, but the actual feedback wasn't the point. We felt that by being completely transparent, we would build more trust with the people in the organization because they would see we weren't hiding anything.

Information radiators are an extremely effective practice for getting all of your thoughts out of your brain and up on a wall. Sometimes we

would leave our Insights up on the wall without acting on them because we weren't sure what to do. When we'd review that same Insight a couple of weeks later, the next Experiment became obvious.

Anonymous feedback via the Insights door helps people feel safe.

Practice 2: Lean Coffee

The week I started working at The Commission I wanted to setup Lean Coffee sessions so that I could gain Insights into how people were feeling about the changes. Anger, uncertainty and frustration are at their peak in the early stages of change. All change management models highlight the value of communication, and Lean Coffee is a perfect way to maximize the communication during this time. It helps provide honest dialog, which creates urgency, and reduces the symptom of resistance.

As I mentioned in Chapter 3, the Lean Coffee sessions provided a low-cost and high value Option for collecting Insights. To get started, all I had to do was print out a sign to let people know where and when the Lean Coffee sessions would happen.

There was no formal meeting invite.

Lean Coffee was the practice I selected to help me generate Insights. These Insights helped me figure out what to do next. My intention for starting with Lean Coffee was to learn:

- Who would be our early adopters? Who would be motivated to learn more about Lean and Agile practices?

- What topics would they want to know more about?

- What departments did the early adopters work in?

What is Lean Coffee?

Lean Coffee is a Lean approach to running meetings. The participants drive the agenda of the meeting, which usually has a focus or theme. People new to Lean Coffee are sometimes skeptical of its effectiveness. How can this possibly work? What if no one writes down a question? But after one session, they're sold!

Here's the structure that Lean Coffee meetings typically follow:

1. The facilitator sets up a Kanban board with three columns: To Discuss, Discussing, and Discussed.

2. The facilitator states the theme, or primary topic. Participants write down questions related to that topic on sticky notes until their brain is empty. It's a good idea to have a time limit of 5-10 minutes just in case there are lots of questions rattling around up there!

3. All of the topics are posted on a wall, or on the table, duplicates are removed, and similar items are merged into a conversation backlog.

4. The backlog of questions is read aloud and, if necessary, the person who wrote the question can expand on it briefly.

5. In order to decide on which topics to talk about first, everyone is given two votes, and they vote by marking the sticky note with a dot. Some people use stickers, however, in the interest of time, drawing a dot on the sticky note is fine. The sticky note that receives the most votes is pulled into the Discussing column. The remaining sticky notes are arranged in the To Discuss column based on priority.

6. Each topic is discussed for a set time, often five minutes. After that time, people vote to either continue the discussion for another two minutes: A thumb up for Yes, thumb sideways for Neutral, and thumb down for No.

In addition to Lean Coffee being a trigger for the creation of the business analysis community of practice (BA CoP), Executive Lean Coffee and the connection to the PMO, it also led to interest in doing book study groups.

One study group read and discussed Johanna Rothman's *Managing Your Project Portfolio* book. The entire PMO participated, and that allowed us to help them mature their practice with Agile and Lean portfolio management concepts. We also had Johanna Rothman join our study group one time via Skype, which motivated the participants more than any of us in the QMO team could ever do!

Lean Coffee gave us a forum to have open and honest dialogue with many people at The Commission. I don't think we could have planned all the outcomes Lean Coffee led to upfront.

Another side benefit to Lean Coffee is that I created our Outreach Program as a result. This program helped me put more effort into socializing Agile and Lean practices throughout the organization, which provided the same benefits on a larger scale that Lean

Coffee did on a smaller scale. That included having Agile thought-leaders present evening sessions at our office, telling stories at The Commission's quarterly town hall meetings, and posting success stories on our Kanban board.

Practice 3: Culture Hacking

A few months into the Kanban transformation at The Commission, we planned to create open-space, co-located working areas. This would allow cross-functional project teams to sit together and collaborate. We knew the people who had to give up the comfort, and privacy, of their cubes weren't going to be happy about it. They had no input into the design of the space, and their new desks were a bit smaller than what they had in their cubes. The developers who were moving in were afraid they would lose their dual-monitor setup because it didn't look like there was enough space on the desks for them. After chasing down countless people from directors to managers to facilities people, I was assured the dual-monitor setup would be kept.

Come moving day, it was as bad as you thought it would be.

The misery at the water cooler was astounding! People were forced to move to a much smaller desk, half of their equipment was missing, and there was nothing anyone could do – *"It's Facility's problem."* No one, including me, knew who was responsible for fixing the problem because there were people from multiple departments sitting together. Employees complained to their managers, but the managers didn't know what to do.

Should the development manager only solve the problem for her developers? What about the testers? What about the project managers and analysts?

I will never forget the meetings with the directors and managers where we were discussing the political and logistical mess of getting a monitor moved! While I'm making fun of the situation now, this is a great example of an organizational dysfunction *from my perspective*. I thought it was ridiculous, but from the directors' and managers' perspective, it was a nightmare. They needed to use existing processes to fix the problem, and they were having a hard time doing that.

I decided all this talk wasn't working. Time for an intervention! It was time to hack the culture.

What is Culture Hacking?

Culture Hacking [2] was introduced to the Agile community by Stefan Haas. I was skeptical when I first heard the term, but after attending Stefan's session on culture hacking at the LESS 2012 conference, I was sold!

DISRUPTIVE INNOVATION IS GOOD. DISRUPTION FOR THE SAKE OF DISRUPTION IS NOT.

I think of culture as a collection of the behaviors and interactions between people in organizations. Trying to understand organizational culture isn't something you can do through analysis alone. Sometimes to truly understand an organization, you have to disrupt it in such a way that provokes a response.

Culture hacking is a practice that has three components: the Crack, the Hack, and the Hacking Zones.

The Crack

A Crack is an organizational dysfunction that feels uncomfortable. Going back to the moving example, managers had no idea how to address a Facilities issue because having cross-functional teams sitting together was a new concept for them. Sounds ridiculous to me, and maybe even to you, but they didn't see the problem as a dysfunction. To them, it was the status quo. Each manager was responsible for their people, not for teams that included people from multiple departments.

The Crack generates tension, friction, frustration, or bad vibes. It may be something you can express in terms of conflicting goals in the organization, erroneous assumptions, or unexpressed feelings that could be revealed by, or serve as leverage for the hack, which is what comes next.

The Hack

The Hack is the action you take to expose, jam, complicate, disrupt, or otherwise point out the crack to the organization. It's a minimal, artful intervention, which if successful, exploits the crack to influence the culture of an organization. You've probably heard people say *"Well, that's just the way things are around here"*. The Hack is something you do to expose the reality that you see to the people who simply see the status quo. By exposing that reality in a tactful way, you'll open their eyes and make them aware of the dysfunction.

Here's a quick culture hacking tip you can use in your organization at your next meeting. Tired of people checking their phone during meetings? Bring a cardboard box to the next meeting you're facilitating labeled *"Temporary Phone Storage"*. Tell people they have a choice. They can put their phone in the box and participate in the meeting or leave!

Here's a riskier hack, bring Monopoly money to your next meeting and start paying participants by performance in the meeting to

Visible, anonymous feedback to help employees raise issues safely.

expose a dysfunctional end-of-year bonus program!

The crack is the dysfunction you see of people not paying attention in meetings because they're too busy checking their phones. The hack is the cardboard box and the policy of telling people to put their phone in the box or leave.

Back to my hack. My Hack for the move problem, which I learned from a fellow coach and friend, Michael Sahota, was to set up a big, visible feedback wall at the entrance of the co-located working area.

This allowed people who weren't comfortable in the space to give honest feedback, anonymously, and it allowed the QMO to give managers the opportunity to do something about it. The feedback helped us design the next co-located working space. So the visible feedback wall was a Hack that successfully exploited the Crack to improve the organization. The Crack being the dysfunction of allowing a ridiculous process to get in the way of making sure staff had everything they needed in their new work area.

Hacking Zones
When designing your Hack, be mindful of the impact. Hacks fit into one of three hacking zones:

- **Green Zone (Safe)**: Think of these Hacks as a gentle kick-in-the-organizational-butt that will safely help an organization become self-aware. They are the least disruptive.

- **Blue Zone (Risky)**: These Hacks can get you hauled into the boss' office for a lecture (or worse!) and result in the opposite effect you were trying to achieve because people will react strongly to them.

- **Red Zone (Dangerous)**: These Hacks are the most disruptive and can lead to you potentially needing to update your résumé. They can also severely harm the company. Perhaps worse, they can result in labelling the change team a bunch of rogues.

I thought the feedback wall was a Green Zone hack, but I was hauled into my boss' office because some people were upset. Apparently – and this is an Insight the Hack revealed – it was not acceptable to make employee discontent with a management decision visible at The Commission. The feedback wall turned out to be a Blue Zone hack – definitely worth doing, but I took some flak for trying it.

Naturally, it would be excellent to know in advance which zone you're in when you design the Hack, but given the complexity of organizations often you'll only find out only after you do it!

Culture hacking is a powerful Experiment you can use to generate Insights. Whether you're following a rigid, plan-driven change process or going with the flow, it can help you understand how to navigate the messiness of organizational change.

Practice 4: Agile Retrospectives

The managers at The Commission were all great people, passionate and protective of the people in their functional areas. At times, they were just as confused and frustrated as the staff was. Through our Insight collection, we learned that the staff was reluctant to give their managers feedback about how they were adjusting to the Kanban transformation. Instead, they were coming to me and the other coaches in the QMO.

I facilitated a few Agile retrospectives with a few teams, and then a separate retrospective with their managers. The key here was that I used the same retrospective format, so I could compare what staff and managers felt was working well and what wasn't.

What is a Retrospective?

If you're unfamiliar with what a retrospective is, it's a meeting the team holds after each work cycle on Agile projects. These work cycles are typically called Sprints or Iterations. After each cycle the team reflects on what worked well and what didn't, and what may need to be changed going forward. For more info on retrospective approaches, read *Agile Retrospectives* by Esther Derby and Diana Larson [3].

I used the *happy, sad, mad* format for these retrospectives. People in the retrospective write the things that made them happy, sad and mad on sticky notes. They then categorize the results, look for patterns, and finally decide what action to take to solve a problem.

I did this with a few project teams at The Commission and brought the result to the manager retrospective. I covered the staff's results with flip-chart paper, ran the retrospective with the managers, and then we talked about the similarities and differences. Some managers had no idea how some of their staff was feeling about aspects of the changes that were happening.

This exercise gave the managers Insights into what they needed to change, and it helped me provide harsh feedback in a safe way. My goal was to expose how staff felt so the managers would be aware and able to react.

Agile retrospectives are a powerful practice for understanding the current reality. Frequent feedback through this practice increases communication and transparency. Transparency can go a long way into shaping future changes, as well as creating mutual understanding and raising trust within the organization.

Practice 5: Kurt Lewin Force Field Analysis [4]

Change resistance is often cited as a reason for why change initiatives fail. We know people will resist change. Force Field analysis is a good practice you can use to help you figure out what's working against the change, and what is working to support it. This, in turn, will generate valuable Insights that you can turn into Options and Experiments.

Kurt Lewin was a social psychologist working in the 1940s who was, in many ways, the pioneer of organizational psychology and change management. He started the change management field by being the first person to describe change as a three-phase journey [4]. One of his practices is called Force Field Analysis. It's a simple technique that can be very helpful for making sense of what happens during a change process.

Force Field Analysis can be done on one sheet of paper. Draw a line down the middle to represent the change you want to introduce. On one side, write all of the forces pushing against or *Restraining* the change. On the other side, write all the forces supporting or *Driving* the change. If you like, assign each force a strength score (e.g. score them 1 to 5, from weak to strong). Add up the results, and you can see the overall force operating on the change, and which direction is strongest: Driving or Restraining.

While writing this book, I began helping another organization use these practices. After their overall transformation strategy was created, our change team used a Force Field Analysis to have the teams feed information back to the executives about what they thought was driving the change, and what was restraining it. This is why Lean Change Management is referred to as a feedback-driven approach to change. This feedback was critical to adjusting the plan, after all, no one knows best what to improve than the people doing the work! Once we had this data, we looked for patterns to figure out what Options and Experiments to do next.

Top-down change without honest feedback from those affected by the change simply will not work. By using this practice, we provided a safe feedback mechanism for teams because the data was anonymous, and we provided the executives with useful information they could use to adjust the strategy.

ASSESSMENTS THAT GENERATE INSIGHTS

Assessments are more formal approaches for generating Insights such as surveys, or traditional change management and culture assessment tools. These assessments provide valuable Insights, but they do require a great deal of data analysis! I'll focus on explaining 3 different types of assessments:

- Prosci ADKAR®
- OCAI Cultural Assessment
- Schneider Culture model

What is AKDAR®?

Procsi's ADKAR® method can be used as a standalone method, and it's probably the most popular change management method today. Many companies follow this method because they find it logical and straightforward.

ADKAR® has two dimensions. The Business dimension and the People dimension. The ADKAR acronym itself refers to the people dimension. The business dimension is composed of four steps.

1. **Business need:** the business need and opportunity are identified.

2. **Concept and Design:** creating the plan for a change process, including scope and objectives.

3. **Implementing:** Executing the change.

4. **Post-implementation:** This step is comprised of the usual project post-implementation activities like project close-out and post-mortem.

Where ADKAR® falls apart for me is the deceptively simple, and linear, nature of those 4 steps. Prosci warns of this in their literature. Once you've created *Awareness* and *Desire,* that doesn't mean everyone in the organization is at the same level and they're ready to acquire *Knowledge.* I fear the simplicity of how this model is described makes facilitating change seem linear and predictable. As a guideline, yes, those steps make logical sense but in implementation, change doesn't follow a neat and tidy path.

The ADKAR® assessment can be a valuable tool for understanding the current reality at the start of an organizational change. That said, once you send out the ADKAR® survey, your reality has changed! It'll take time to analyze the results and by then, the reality will be different.

Imagine receiving a survey about a big change you knew nothing about. The first thing I would do is ask colleagues about it at lunch, or at the water-cooler. We'd make our assumptions about the change and draw our own conclusions before the change team started implementing it!

That's what I mean about how change agents are always stepping into a constantly changing reality. Planning alone cannot manage that complexity.

How the Commission Used ADKAR®

The change management team we worked with at The Commission executed the ADKAR® assessment. This was my first experience with the method so I was interested to see what Insights we would generate with it. After the survey and analysis, the change management team came to the following conclusions:

- The Desire to change at the staff level was high.
  (D – dimension in ADKAR®)

- The managers had a favorable opinion of their staff to execute the changes.
  (A – Ability in ADKAR®)

- The directors had a less-than-favorable opinion of the managers to perform the changes.
  (Also referring to Ability.)

Now that we knew the *Desire* to change was high at the staff level, we could prepare for more training and information sessions because we knew that they would be welcome. In fact, the demand for our coaching and training services increased quickly, and we found ourselves being spread too thin at times.

The QMO, anticipated that we would have challenges at the director level because the results pointed to their less-than-favorable opinion of their managers' *Ability* to implement the changes. The main challenges we faced at the director level were apathy and misalignment. A couple of the directors was motivated to help this change succeed but as a leadership team, they weren't actively involved most of the time.

While the ADKAR® results didn't indicate any lack of alignment, our gut feel led us to the conclusion (assumption?) we would have some challenges at the director level. To be blunt, something felt off about how they rated their managers. Practices and assessments aren't the only way to generate Insights, your experience and gut feel also play a role.

On the flip-side, the results showed us the relationship between managers and staff was strong, as indicated by the managers' high opinion of their staff to implement the changes.

OCAI – Organizational Culture Assessment Instrument [5]

"You can't do Agile, you have to be Agile!" was the cutesy slogan written on the whiteboard at the Agile conference I spoke at in 2013. Next to that statement was another gem, *"Agile is a mindset, you have to change your culture!"*

There is a strong bias with many Agile practitioners about the need for a culture and mindset change with respect to Agile. I see the same stance from people in the business community when they talk about innovation. I'm sure you've seen many posts and forum discussions about how culture will eat your strategy for breakfast.

This makes perfect sense for people who have their biases confirmed by these statements. For others though, changing culture and mindsets starts with more well defined processes, because they believe better processes will help them.

Regardless of what your point of view is, there are tools for measuring and managing culture. You have to decide if you want to make a conscious attempt to change the organization's culture, which determines whether or not to use a culture assessment tool. If you try an approach that isn't compatible with your culture, you could cause more harm than good, or worse, ruin your credibility as a change agent.

The OCAI model describes four culture types:

- **Clan**: Internally focused, values flexibility and freedom

- **Hierarchy:** Internally focused, values stability and control

- **Adhocracy:** Externally focused, values flexibility and freedom

- **Market:** Externally focused, values stability and control

The main concept underlying the OCAI model is the Competing Values Framework. This framework is referred to as a sense-making device that helps leaders understand how to manage the simultaneous harmony and tension that occurs within organizations. The reference section at the end of this book lists more resources about this framework if you'd like to learn more [6, 7, 8].

While the QMO didn't use a formal culture assessment tool, the behaviors we observed were in line with what you would see in a Hierarchy culture. In the Agile community, practitioners often use the statement *"command and control"* to describe the behavior where managers set and enforce the rules in a top-down fashion. Learning about how to recognize different cultures by understanding attributes of each can be helpful in figuring out what approach to take for introducing change.

The benefit of understanding what makes a Hierarchy culture tick helped us become more aware of the norms in the organization. Some of these included learning about the un-spoken processes for traversing the hierarchy, to knowing that control and process were strongly held values. Sometimes we would shape our changes as new process so we could speak the language of The Commission's unique culture.

Schneider Culture Model

William Schneider describes four cultures in his book The *Re-Engineering Alternative: A Plan for Making Your Current Culture Work* [9] that are similar to OCAI's cultures:

- **Collaboration:** *"We succeed by working together"*
  (people and reality oriented)

- **Control:** *"We succeed by establishing and maintaining control"*
  (company and reality oriented)

- **Cultivation:** *"We succeed by growing our people"*
  (people and possibility oriented)

- **Competence:** *"We succeed by being the best"*
  (company and reality oriented)

Schneider describes how each of these cultures aligns with psychology types described by Carl Jung, and that organizational culture emerges from the personality types of its leaders. For example, if the CEO of your organization reacts aggressively to every problem and wants to create new processes to deal with the problem, a control culture is likely to emerge and spread throughout.

Schneider is clear in his book that one culture is not better than any other – they're just different. Some people feel a control culture is bad. It's not, it just depends on the organization. At its best, a control culture can operate like a well-oiled machine. At its worst, progress in grinds to halt when rules and bureaucracy throttle everything.

Each of the four cultures has their strengths and weaknesses. Once you recognize the symptoms of each, you will be more likely to pick Options that have a better chance to work with a specific team or organization.

The practices and assessments outlined in this chapter can be used to generate Insights about the current reality you, as a change agent, are facing. You just need to learn how to choose the right practice or assessment, at the right time, that's right for your organization. That's the fun part of being a change agent! At least for me.

While I find that fun, some can find that challenging. While writing this chapter, I was conducting a book study group on the first edition of this book with the organizational effectiveness team at a Fortune 100 company. One of the practitioners was having a hard time figuring out where to start a new initiative he was assigned to. This initiative had the possibility to effect thousands of people. Or at least he thought it would.

He was worried about involving too many, or not enough, people in the design of the change and felt stuck, as far as creating *the plan*. After a couple of sessions, the ideas behind Insights clicked for him. He recognized that Insights are being generated constantly by interacting with people in the organization, even while executing the change plan. It's that real-time feedback that helps you, as the change agent, to make sense of the constantly evolving reality.

In the end, he decided to use a Lean Coffee session and a big visible wall to create awareness about the change. The next challenge becomes running a Lean Coffee at this scale. With distributed people! The jury is still out about what happened, but there will be bonus material released along with this book so don't worry, you'll find out what happened!

Now that you've filled your brain with Insights, what's next? How can you make sense of this sometimes overwhelming data? You'll probably have many ideas for what to do. Which one is the right one to start with?

In the next chapter, I'll show you how to answer those questions!

5
FRAMEWORKS

MAKING SENSE OF INSIGHTS

5. FRAMEWORKS

"You guys didn't move our Kanban board!" the project manager accused me and the QMO.

That moment was identified during a project closeout as THE point when the project went off the rails. As you can imagine, this particular project didn't end well. The team was exhausted and frustrated, but eventually managed to finish the project – 6 months late and littered with defects but it was finished.

This team had been sitting together in an open-space working area, and about halfway through the project, they moved to another area of the building. However, they didn't take their Kanban board with them. They had been using it to visualize their work. Without the board present in their new work area, they stopped doing daily stand-up meetings to co-ordinate their work, which lead to all the delays and obstacles. They decided that it was the missing Kanban board that led to the unraveling of the project.

Really?

No, let me ask again: REALLY?

How can it be that I, their coach, caused their project to end the way it did by not moving three LOUSY pieces of flip chart paper to their new workspace?

My brain said, *"That is THE DUMBEST excuse for a failed project I've ever heard!"* But by the time the sound waves escaped from my vocal cords, something in between my brain and my mouth translated that to, *"Oh, I didn't realize that was something we were expected to do!"*

I experienced a few similar events during my time at The Commission, and I came to this realization: people at The Commission expected the Kanban transformation to be something *those change people do*.

Events like this gave me the impression that some people didn't feel *they* owned the change. Perhaps that had to do with how the external consultants were pushing the changes. Perhaps I, and the QMO team, did a poor job of setting expectations. Perhaps that is what the CIO expected us to do all along.

Without a framework, or some mental model of the bigger picture, change teams can end up fumbling around in the dark doing one-off actions that aren't stitched together in a larger context. Ownership of the change by the people affected by the change speaks to a sense of urgency, which is the first step in one of the frameworks I'll describe next.

FRAMEWORKS

Kotter's 8-Step Change Model [1]

Dr. John Kotter describes an 8-step process for leading change in his book, *Leading Change*:

1. Create Urgency
2. Form a Powerful Coalition
3. Create a Vision for the Change
4. Communicate the Vision
5. Remove Obstacles
6. Create Short Term Wins
7. Build on the Change
8. Anchor the Change in Corporate Culture

Create Urgency

The first step for leading change is to create urgency. In the case of The Commission, the CIO had already decided that IT was going Agile. His definition of urgency was completing a 3-year modernization program. The consulting firm already decided that Kanban was the methodology that was to be used. Their urgency was ensuring the adoption of these practices by the end date in their consulting proposal. The QMO's urgency was similar to the consulting team's urgency, except we knew we'd be around after they left. We knew there would be much more work to do when the change project was done. My point is, urgency is a matter of perspective. While the CIO, external consultants and us, the QMO, had different perspectives of the urgency, we were all looking towards the same end state, namely a more stable, and predictable delivery of software.

URGENCY FOR CHANGE EMERGES THROUGH HONEST DIALOGUE BETWEEN PEOPLE WITH DIFFERENT POINTS OF VIEW

Figuring out the urgency from the staff's point of view was a bit more difficult. In order to sustain the change, we knew that we had to discover the true sense of urgency for them. Otherwise, the staff would feel like they're too busy to focus on important work because everything is an emergency. Busyness and busy-work are common symptoms of false urgency.

In Lean Change Management, urgency emerges by involving the people affected by the change in the design of the change. It starts with open and honest dialogue.

The Lean Coffee Experiment I mentioned in Chapter 3 is an example of how to keep open and honest dialogue happening. Through that informal, but structured, conversation, we were able to understand the perspective of the staff at The Commission.

Form a Powerful Coalition

Kotter refers to this step as *"creating a team of change agents and evangelists that facilitate the change"*. He recommends that team members on the coalition should rotate every so often in order to bring a fresh perspective about the change. At The Commission, the official Powerful Coalition was the QMO and the external consultants. What was missing was having other internal employees be part of this coalition. I say this in retrospect because another organization I worked with had an internal group called a Change Champions group. This group was comprised of employees who were supporting the change, but who were not part of the core transformation team. These employees were people who either wanted help with the change, or wanted to become change agents themselves. As a consultant in that organization, this shows me there *is* urgency to change because people are volunteering to help. More importantly, it shows the organization is owning the change and not relying on me to push it through.

Had we rotated people in and out of the QMO at The Commission, we may have seen more ownership from the people affected by the change.

I hoped that the Lean Coffee sessions would help us find early adopters who could eventually become part of this coalition, but that didn't work.

Kotter says this Powerful Coalition must have capability to lead change, and the clout in the organization to get things done. The QMO had a great deal of experience in managing Agile transformations. We also had direct access to the CIO, which gained us influence. However, it wasn't enough. We didn't have enough support and clout, in the middle layer of the organization. That's important because it's middle management that has the clout to support, or squash, tactical actions for implementing changes. Their staff members are more likely to take direction from them as opposed to listening to the external consultants and us.

Here's what I mean: The Kanban transformation was bringing lighter-weight project management processes, and artifacts with it. One of the managers of the Project Managers, however, was still asking project managers for the big, heavy documents. We in the QMO however, were asking those same project managers to not produce them.

Despite getting agreement with this manager about how project management would be different in the new world, we didn't see him supporting this agreement with his actions.

Create a Vision for the Change

Think of the vision as your 30-second elevator pitch for the change. This vision must be specific, measurable, actionable, inspiring and realistic. Our vision, as handed down from the CIO, was to become *"the best public sector organization in Canada"*. This was a difficult vision to rally around because The Commission was the only game in town. It didn't matter what we did, we were *"the best"* by default. The people who used The Commission's services didn't have a choice.

We, in the QMO, created a vision for our team based on how we could contribute to The Commission becoming *"the best public sector organization in Canada"*. Instead of creating a written vision statement, we created a visual representation of our vision: a lighthouse.

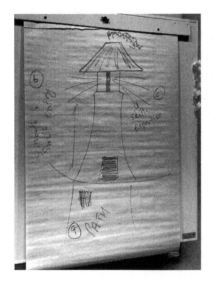

Metaphors are more effective than text vision statements.

We presented our vision at a department meeting to explain that our responsibility was to help guide people, or light the path, so to speak, in the adoption of Lean and Agile software practices.

Perhaps the light in the lighthouse made light bulbs turn on in their heads! This picture helped us spark conversations with the people in the organization who gave us great feedback. They said it helped them understand how the QMO could help them and, more importantly, that we were a supporting function, not a controlling one.

Using the lighthouse picture and metaphor worked well for us. I highly recommend creating something visual as opposed to a text-only statement. A study conducted by Childers & Houston [3] in 1984 concluded that people were 58% more likely to recall details about combined pictures and words versus written words alone.

Communicate the Vision

After we created our lighthouse vision (and perhaps because of it), our department director decided to create an overall department vision.

Each functional group in the department drew something to represent the department vision, and then we voted on which one captured the essence of what our department was responsible for. The act of going through this exercise created alignment within the department, and it was much more powerful way to communicate our department's vision. I highly recommend doing this exercise with your change team, simply for the conversation the picture will generate!

I thought it was interesting how, during this exercise, some managers told their staff to just draw a lighthouse! Apparently our metaphor was a powerful one and perhaps more powerful than the vision statement the CIO came up with. I mentioned the CIO's vision earlier in this chapter; do you remember it? ☺

Remove Obstacles

During the transition, people need to know they are being supported through the change process. Managers and executives can show their support by addressing concerns of the people directly affected by the change.

In the photocopy room that served as our nerve center at The Commission, we posted risks, issues, and blockers for IT projects and the Kanban transformation itself on the wall using sticky notes. Directors, managers, project managers, and interested observers would meet in front of this big visible wall three times per week and co-ordinate resolution activities.

While we didn't solve every problem all the time, the process of using big visible information radiators, as well as meeting frequently created high transparency and improved communication between people in different departments.

People need to feel they are supported while working through change. By making all our problems visible, and tracking new, in progress, and done issues, everyone gets to see that progress is being made.

Create Short Term Wins

This step addresses the risk of people falling back into old habits if they don't see quick wins or immediate benefits. One way we recognized short-term wins at The Commission was to implement a Kudo wall, which is a practice from Management 3.0 [4]. A Kudo wall is simply a space where we posted thank you notes, called Kudo cards, to show people we appreciated the work they did. Here's a picture of our Kudo wall.

We felt it was important to recognize that people were working hard to learn new processes as a result of the Kanban transformation. Early on, all the Kudo cards were written by the QMO to reward the positive behaviors we observed. Over time, other people started rewarding their co-workers. These seemingly small actions almost always have a tremendous, positive impact on re-enforcing the change.

The trick with this step is to not sacrifice the longer-term vision by *only* focusing on short-term gains. Short-term wins help keep people motivated to push through the pain of change. They project a positive view of progress towards the longer-term vision is being made.

Build on the Change

Once you've experienced small wins, it's time to amplify their impact. You can do this in many different ways. One experiment we wanted to run was to bring in early adopters from

Thank you notes make people happy!

different departments into the QMO. We felt that the early adopters, who experienced success with these new practices, could help us amplify the adoption with other people and teams. At one of the BA Community of Practice (BA CoP) meetings, one of the analysts presented their story about using a new practice for creating software requirements. She said, *"I'm not sure if we did the practice right, but the business really liked it!"* It would have been fantastic to bring her into our team and help her evolve into a coach that would go on to lead the change process later. However transferring people from one department to another at The Commission was a bureaucratic nightmare. We decided to try something else instead.

The Commission held quarterly town hall meetings, so we thought we'd encourage staff to present their successes with these new practices. That adds more credibility to the change because real people on real projects were talking about real results. Not only did it motivate the team that saw real results, it motivated other teams to try these practices because they now had a mental picture of how those practices could be applied at The Commission.

Anchor the Change in Corporate Culture

This is the infamous culture change, or mindset shift, I mentioned while describing the OCAI and Schneider culture assessment tools in Chapter 4. Once people have incorporated the changes into their new self, the new processes become the way we work. People are no longer consciously applying new practices; they just do it. Kotter says the culture shift comes last, not first. That means the changes need to prove to people in the organization that they work before the utopian culture shift occurs.

Organizational changes, like the ones The Commission was going through, were designed to improve organizational performance. Performance increases aren't necessarily the result of a culture change.

For example, in a culture that values stability and control, optimizing process and stripping out bureaucracy can improve performance. That doesn't mean the culture has migrated to one that doesn't value stability and control. It also doesn't mean people in the organization made a mindset shift (or changed their overall culture). It simply means the organization is performing better because they learned how to improve the attributes of their existing culture.

Some will say that's a culture shift. That is not the case. It simply means they've anchored the change in their existing culture. In an organization that values control and process, optimizing those processes by cutting out red tape doesn't mean a culture change. To that organization, it means process optimization.

As an example, I didn't observe a radical shift to an Agile mindset at The Commission. What I did see was extremely painful daily standup meetings in front of our EKB. After a while, those standup meetings became the norm. That change was anchored into the culture, but the culture was still one of process and control.

McKinsey 7S Framework [2]

The consultants working at The Commission brought a practice for creating software requirements called Behaviour Driven Development, or BDD for short. In the Agile world, this is an advanced practice, and it's really hard to do right, even for experienced Agile practitioners.

The challenge to applying this practice was that, at The Commission, we had low maturity level for creating ANY sort of requirements. Jumping to an advanced practice, such as BDD, was too big of a leap for people, because they hadn't learned the intermediary step first. The intermediary step is learning how to create requirements through collaboration between business analysts, developers, testers, and customers. The good intention of introducing BDD created a wide-sweeping domino effect that we couldn't have anticipated.

Business Analysts stopped using ANY of the practices they had previously been using to understand and breakdown requirements. Instead, they started *writing BDD's*. Business stakeholders didn't like this, and still wanted their big requirements documents. The QMO and PMO teams were stuck right in the middle, trying to bridge the gap between the two groups. And if that wasn't complex enough, the PMO still had to deal with a government regulatory issue related to project documentation. The simple act of moving to a new requirements creation practice ended up being a lot more complex than was originally thought.

As you can imagine, this *"small"* change within IT created many ripples throughout the organization forcing people outside the team to change what they were doing as well.

This type of domino effect is exactly what the 7S framework describes – how a change in one area of an organization has consequences in other areas. This change to using BDD's wasn't something that could be done in isolation. Had we used the 7S framework as a guide to validate our Experiment, we may have been more prepared to manage the ripple effects of this change.

Tom Peters and Bob Waterman created the 7S framework in the 1980s. At that time, when people talked about organizations, they mostly focused on structure. Peters and Waterman pointed out that if you wanted to diagnose and solve organizational problems, you needed to think about more than just the structure. They identified six other related factors, which they considered to be just as important: Strategy, Systems, Skills, Style, Staff, and Shared values (called "Superordinate goals" in early versions of the model).

Peters and Waterman described some of these factors as "hard" and others as "soft". "Hard" factors are tangible factors that can be easily defined, while "soft" factors are the more ambiguous and complex factors.

This framework tells you that if you change one of the seven factors, it impacts the others. You have to manage those impacts, and make additional changes to bring all seven elements into alignment again.

Throughout my research for this book, I learned that 7S is less popular compared to the more linear, step-by-step models and frameworks. Most of the comments I read, and conversations I had resulted in people believing that it was too complex to be actionable.

HARD FACTORS	SOFT FACTORS
STRATEGY STRUCTURE SYSTEMS	SHARED VALUES SKILLS STYLE STAFF

For me, that's one of the reasons it is one of the best frameworks for Change Management: it accepts the interconnectedness of today's organizations, instead of trying to manage that interconnectedness with simple, and linear models.

The introduction of Agile amplifies the complexity of interconnected organizations. When IT adopts a radically different way for implementing projects and focuses on earlier delivery and cross-functional teams, the business must change their strategy and structure to match. When that doesn't happen, friction between IT and the business is amplified.

That friction leads to more separation between IT and the business and ultimately leads to the organization sliding back into the old way of doing things.

SUMMARY OF FRAMEWORKS

The frameworks I present here are the air-traffic control component of Lean Change Management. Without them, you're left with stumbling around poking people with sticks in the dark.

Kotter's Eight Steps: Think of Kotter's eight steps as the list of ingredients that go into a successful change recipe. But don't go through the steps in a linear way like an actual recipe. Instead, treat them as a guide. A guide that helps you navigate the messy process that change really is.

I use Kotter's framework as a checklist of sorts. I want to make sure I'm addressing the concerns of all eight steps through a variety of methods and practices.

McKinsey's 7S: McKinsey's 7S is a powerful framework I use to map out the dynamic elements of change and anticipate the ripples each change will create. I use this framework in a stealth way. When someone recommends we need to change a process, I now ask, *"If we change this, what other areas of the organization might be affected?"*

By themselves, these frameworks don't tell you *how* to go about planning and implementing change programs. But rather, simply, they do help you understand how interconnected today's organizations are and what element must be present in your change strategy. For execution, you need to combine the practices and assessments from Chapter 4. This is where the Lean Change Management model shines, through its cycle of Insights, Options, and Experiments. Through this cycle, you can use any method, process or practice to "feed" the Lean Change Management model.

By now you're probably exhausted and feeling over model-ified! I know that it can be difficult to know where to start when faced with large change programs. Traditional thinking says that you must follow a process and create a plan. Lean Change Management says, collect Insights first in order to guide and shape your process and plan.

That's the big difference.

The Onirik study I cited in Chapter 1 concluded that the lack of a structured change process is one reason why change initiatives fail. That's not the case. Trying to apply a structured change process is one of the *causes*. Lean Change Management will help you build your own change process that is adapted to your organization's reality. The process you create and follow will evolve over time as you learn how your organization reacts to change.

The frameworks I mentioned in this chapter, combined with the practices and assessments I mentioned in Chapter 4 are the ingredients that you use to create your own change process.

> TRYING TO APPLY A STRUCTURED CHANGE PROCESS IS ONE OF THE CAUSES OF CHANGE FAILURES

The Insights you generate by using the frameworks, practices and assessments I've mentioned over the last two chapters will be inputs into your change plan. In the next chapter, I'll show you how to take those Insights and turn them into Options that will drive your next steps in managing change.

6
OPTIONS

SHAPING YOUR CHANGE PLAN

6. OPTIONS

"You know what, never mind. It's not going to work, so let's figure out something else."

"You're right John. I haven't seen a solitary enterprise product backlog work in an organization of this size," I replied. *"I think we have more important Options to sort out first."*

And with that conversation, an extremely high-cost and questionably-valued Option was thrown into the Abandon All Hope bucket. The purpose of this Option was to help deal with the project prioritization problem. Most projects involved 10-20 teams, and the idea was to have all these teams share a solitary list of priorities. We decided it was far too big of a problem to solve given we were only a few months into this organization's Agile transformation. Option discarded.

I'm sure you've been involved in more brainstorming meetings and water cooler conversations that generate more awesome ideas than you can remember. Options *kinda* start out that way. They start out with statements like: "It might not be a bad idea if we..." The intent is to start thinking about how to solve problems you, as a change agent, have observed.

At The Commission, the QMO met weekly to discuss Options. Many of our Options started out as a "you know, I think this would work..." idea. These Options were based on Insights we collected through interviews, retrospectives, surveys, and our observations. It was during this meeting where we'd start our problem solving process.

There are many approaches to problem solving. One approach is to use tools from the Lean world, like 5 Why's, and root-cause analysis, which are great for exploring the problem. The theory is that by lingering in the problem space, you understand the problem better and only then can you come up with the right solutions.

Another approach is to focus on solutions. Some feel this is a better approach because it relies on thinking about a future state where the problem doesn't exist, rather than dwelling on the problem. This is called solution-focused thinking, and it has its roots in the therapeutic approach called Solution-Focused Brief Therapy [1] (SFBP) devised by Steve de Shazer and Insoo Kim Burg. According to this theory, change happens when people construct solutions, rather than dwell on problems. The question associated closely with SFBP is referred to as the Miracle Question:

> *"Suppose you went to bed and overnight, a miracle occurred.*
> *What are some of things you would notice that would tell*
> *you things are better?"*

According to SFBP, this question gets people thinking about goals instead of focusing on obstacles, or reasons why the change won't work.

I prefer this solution-focused thinking, and that's the primary method we employed at The Commission. We were transforming to a new state at The Commission, so in some respects, we wanted to ignore the current state, and the reasons why agile "wouldn't" work. In Lean

Change Management, Options are designed to help people take an action that will get them to their desired future state without worrying about the current state. That's the difference between *transformation* and *change*.

- In order to *change* a process, you need to play in the problem space for a while to truly understand it.

- In order to *transform* to a new organizational state, use solution-focused thinking to get to that desired future state.

Hint: If your conversations about Options generate many *"That won't work here because..."* statements, dig deeper into the reasons why you think it won't work. That may help you discover less disruptive Experiments to run.

HOW TO CHOOSE OPTIONS

The term *Options* came from my fellow QMO coach, Andrew Annett. In his view, all changes have a cost and a questionable value, just like stock market options. The other inspiration for it comes from what I learned from Jerry Weinberg: If you only have one option, you have no options. If you have two options, you have a dilemma. When you have three options, only then do you truly have Options.

At this point, all Options are valid, including silly ones, so resist the temptation to throw away ideas that sound a bit crazy In his 2003 study at the University of California, Charlan Nemeth concluded that being exposed to alternate views expands our creative potential. That's because our brains try to make sense of the silly Option, which causes us to re-evaluate our initial assumptions about the problem we're trying to solve.

Here's an example of what I mean.

I ran into a problem at The Commission where people were being sent on traditional "waterfall" project management training. That didn't make sense to me, since we were moving away from those types of practices, and towards Agile and Lean practices. I started thinking about some Options to approach this:

1.   Talk to the sponsoring Director and cancel the training.

2.   Start advertising the QMO's PM training, which of course meant we'd need to build our own course.

3.   Find another vendor to do Agile certification training.

I ruled out the first Option because the Director who brought in the traditional training was the least supportive of these "new" practices. That was a high-cost challenge for me because I didn't have the clout to challenge this Director, so I decided against it.

The second Option was a high-value Option, but the QMO was already stretched pretty thin, so we just couldn't design our own training course.

The third Option made the most sense for a few reasons:
A.   I knew many people in the local Agile community, and a few were offering the Project Management Institute's Agile Certified Practitioner (PMI-ACP) course.

B.   It would be easy for me bring in one of them to teach it.

C.   I thought the people at The Commission would be motivated to gain a new Agile certification through this course.

This Option was high-cost, high-value, and one that was definitely possible to implement.

It was high-cost because I'd have to persuade the Learning & Performance (L&P) team to relax their pass/fail rule for reimbursable training. At The Commission, the L&P team was responsible for training and skills development. This PMI-ACP course was an exam prep course, so there was no test at the end of it. Whoever attended would have to schedule the exam. I'd also have to coordinate the logistics and deal with the vendor. In addition to that, I'd have to sit-in on the training to provide organizational context during the class.The high cost is derived from the amount of time and effort I'd need to spend on this Option.

I thought this Option had high-value because, like it or not, some people are motivated by adding a credential to their Linked In profile! If they're happy and motivated to do the training, and it happens to align with the practices we're introducing, that's high-value in my books!

FACTORS THAT AFFECT YOUR OPTIONS

There are three major factors to consider when assessing your Options:

- **Cost:** What's the effort or investment needed to make this Option viable?

- **Value:** What's the benefit? Does it outweigh the cost?

- **Level of Disruption:** How disruptive would this Option be in the organization? Often this is a gut-feel notion, and hard to quantify.

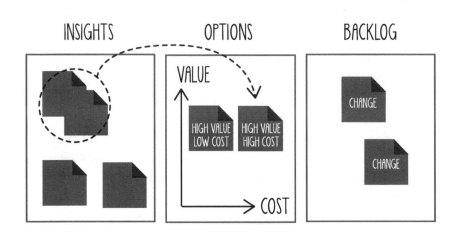

Compare the cost and value of Options.

HOW TO ASSESS YOUR OPTIONS

More than likely you'll have a sense of how difficult some Options will be to implement as you're comparing them. Don't worry about diving into too much detail right away. Plot your Options quickly on a chart so you can see them all at once.

Once you've plotted your Options, do a second pass:

• Highlight Options you think will bring high disruption with a red sticker.

- Using your gut feel, throw any Options you feel might not work yet into the Abandon bucket. Remember, you may want to do them, but now might not be the right time.

- Walk your change sponsor through your thinking and get his/her input.

ALL OPTIONS HAVE A COST

The cost of an Option is mostly related to the effort needed to execute the Option. So why not use effort? I'm using the term *cost* intentionally here because I'm not just talking about the financial cost of an Option. Other than the oodles of money being spent on consultants, there are many *costs* to implementing change:

- **Time spent working on the change:** Changes need to be planned, people in the organization need to be aligned with the change and that takes time. Suppose you're trying to implement a change that affects 7 different departments. That's a hard change to do and it'll take time to get everyone aligned.

- **Developing new capabilities:** Includes hard costs such as training courses or hiring coaches to work with employees.

- **Productivity Drop:** It is difficult to put a dollar value on this item, but it's very real. People need time to practice their newly developed skills, and your overall business may suffer as they incorporate these new capabilities and strategies.

Using the word *cost* helps stakeholders realize that **all** actions in the change plan cost the organization *something*.

Each of the practices, assessments, and framework I mentioned in the previous two chapters has a cost associated with them. For example, consider the cost of accomplishing Kotter's first step, Create Urgency. Urgency doesn't magically happen because of the fancy intranet site you've created to communicate your big change plan! The honest dialogue that is needed to allow urgency to emerge takes people away from their day-to-day work. We used Lean Coffee meetings to facilitate that dialogue. The cost to establish and run the Lean Coffee sessions was mainly time: the time I spent organizing the meetings, the time people spent in the sessions, as well as the time needed to analyze the data we collected from each session.

Another consideration for assessing cost is thinking about the un-intended consequences the Option may bring. Since the McKinsey 7S Framework points out the interconnections between facets of the organization, why not use that framework to try to anticipate chain reactions, and the costs associated with managing those?

Lewin's Force Field Analysis is another way to uncover costs that help mitigate the risk of implementing the wrong changes. If you see strong opposing forces to a particular change, you're going to have a higher cost trying to implement that Option.

All of the change management frameworks in this book help you identify potential costs associated with an Option. The trick is in knowing how, and when, to apply each of them in order to assess the Cost of your Option.

Fortunately, there is a shortcut that will make it much easier to understand the potential cost of your Options. This magic secret will help you think through Options without even needing a deep understanding of all of the frameworks I've already mentioned!

At The Commission, the QMO met weekly to plot new changes on our cost-versus-value chart. When it came time to dig deeper into Options that we thought would be high-cost, we used two specific types of visualization to help us think through the change:

1. **Blast Radius:** Brainstorm and list the intended and possible un-intended consequences of introducing this change. For example, changing status report formats seemed like a trivial change, but since so many departments use and rely on them, it was a hard process to change.

2. **Sphere of Influence Diagram:** How hard would this change be, given who would be affected by it? For example, are the people affected by the change outside our direct sphere of influence? How would they react to someone outside their department suggesting they change how they work? Conversely, how could we leverage people within our sphere of influence to help us implement the change?

UNDERSTANDING THE BLAST RADIUS

Change is unpredictable. Sometimes your good intentions are met with strong, negative reactions. That's why it's a good idea to think about the change first, and map out the consequences of introducing it.

The blast radius is the ripple effect the change will have in the organization. Visualizing the blast radius of the change is extremely important. It helps you think through the overall change plan, and it provides transparency to people affected by the changes. It's a good idea to get your change team in a room and in front of a whiteboard to create this diagram effectively.

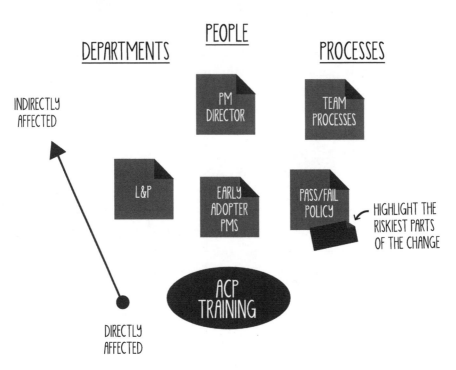

Understand the consequences of change.

Draw the name of the change in the middle of the whiteboard, and ask the team these questions:

> ### Which departments, people, and management roles are directly and indirectly affected by the change?

For example, when I wanted to bring in PMI-ACP training, the L&P team was directly affected because they'd have to change a training policy. The director who brought in the traditional PM training (and who was the project manager's boss), would be indirectly affected. I say "indirectly" because I thought he might not allow 'his people' to go on the new training since it wasn't his idea. And guess what? I was right. The director who brought in the traditional PM training was upset. Some people were allowed to go to the PMI-ACP training, and others weren't, which caused some friction within the PM group.

What processes would be directly and indirectly affected by the change?

For example, the PMI-ACP training would initially be denied because it didn't meet L&P's pass/fail criteria. I knew that a policy I had no control over had to change for the teams to go on this training. The process was being indirectly affected by this change.

Allow me to jump into my time machine and rewind a few months. I had established a relationship with people in the L&P team because the CIO wanted me to run a Management 3.0 course for directors and managers.

When it came time to negotiate the pass/fail policy, I knew who to speak to on the L&P team. I had a solid relationship with the decision makers in the L&P team, and I loved working with them! They shared our vision and stance about developing capability rather than forcing training and process on employees. This shared perspective would become important later.

I relied on my contacts in the L&P team to deal with the processes that would be indirectly affected, namely approval from executives, and the 'official' training policies of the organization. Through some face-to-face discussions, I explained to them why this course was the Kanban transformation. They dealt with all the politics to change the policies to allow non-pass/fail courses to be reimbursed.

While the initial change seems like a simple one, this was a **radical** change for The Commission because, to my knowledge, no one had challenged the pass/fail criteria before. I'm happy it worked out. The people who attended the course were excited, and a couple of them even gained their ACP certification.

USING YOUR SPHERE OF INFLUENCE

Once you know the blast radius of the change, you can use a Sphere of Influence diagram to map out how you can reach influencers for this change At The Commission, the Director of L&P was a strong influencer and so was the Director of the department the QMO reported into. We had direct access to both. Sometimes our influencers were staff members who were considered to be the "go to" people in their department. Whether it be at the staff layer or management layer, influencers are needed to help spread awareness about the change. Without influencers, it can be extremely difficult for people in the change team to get people on board with the change.

Sometimes you may know who the influencer is, but you may not have a direct relationship with them. However, you may know someone who has a relationship with that influencer. The sphere of influence diagram will help you make those connections.

Creating the Diagram

1. Draw a circle in the bottom corner of the whiteboard or flip chart paper to represent the change you're wanting to introduce.

SPHERE OF INFLUENCE

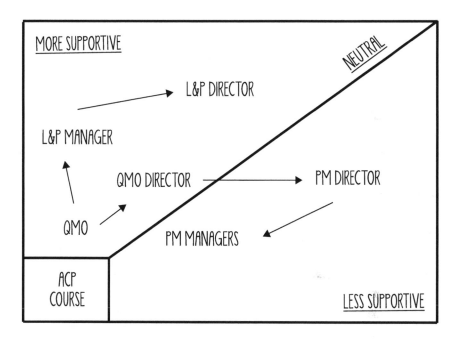

Understand where support will come from.

2. Write the names of influential people on the outer edges of your paper or whiteboard. These are people with the clout to support or kill the change.

3. Using your network of people, draw lines to connect your change to the influencers.

- the QMO had influence with the QMO director

- the QMO had influence with the L&P manager

- the L&P manager had influence with the L&P director who would ultimately need to approve the change to the pass/fail policy

- the QMO director had influence with the PM director

- the PM director had influence with the PM managers

- the PM managers I considered neutral. While they were supportive, they would have to settle with whatever their director decided on

The idea behind the sphere of influence diagram is to understand how hard this change will be. It will also help you gain a better understanding of where the support is (and isn't) for the change. This is a critical insight to help you decide whether to commit to or abandon the change.

CLASSIFYING YOUR OPTIONS

If you've followed the process I outline in this book up to this point, you've generated Insights about your organization, and some Options that consider the unique characteristics of your organization. For those Options, you've considered who is affected, where the support might be, and where the resistance might manifest.

Now consider how these Options fit into your overall change plan by classifying them based on what you're trying to accomplish. Going through this exercise will help you see if you've added all the elements that are needed in any change initiative. In Chapter 5, I mentioned that I use Kotter's 8-steps as a checklist, not a linear process to follow. That applies to the other change methods and frameworks, such as McKinsey 7S and ADKAR® as well:

For example:

- Will this Option contribute to a quick win? (Kotter's 6th Step)

- Is this Option designed to help build urgency? (Kotter's 1st Step)

- If this Option is a change to strategy, how will it affect the other six McKinsey dimensions? (McKinsey 7S)

- Is this Option designed to generate awareness about the change? (ADKAR®)

These are just some of the questions you can use to find out how the Options you're considering fit into the big picture. You can get extra material, including video tutorials and other multimedia content, here: www.leanchange.org/resources

Shameless plug aside, at this point you should start thinking about the order in which you would introduce these changes. At The Commission we used a simple visualization to classify and sequence our Options:

To use this method, take the Options you've generated and start plotting them under the following columns:

- **Do Now:** Place in this column all of the Options you will start working on right away. For example, we needed to arrange training at The Commission.

MANAGING CHANGE WITH KANBAN

	ABANDON	YIKES!	DO LATER	DO NOW
TRAINING			USER STORIES	GET KANBAN
COMMUNICATION		STAKEHOLDERS AT STANDUPS		LE COI NIGHTLY MEETUPS
PROCESS CHANGES	PERFORMANCE REVIEWS	PROJECT FUNDING	X-FUNCTIONAL TEAM PILOT	

Make your change plan visible.

- **Do Later:** These are Options you consider doing in the near future, but might need to be adapted, given how the actions in the **Do Now** column pan out. For example, at The Commission, one Option was to move away from functional teams and towards cross-functional teams. We didn't think this was possible early on given the strong silos, but we knew we wanted to get there eventually, so we kept it in the **Do Later** column. We needed to wait for other changes to run their course before we could execute this one.

- **Yikes, Not Sure:** These are the risky Options. They could have high-cost and questionable value. For example, take our Option to eliminate status reports, and instead have stakeholders participate in the teams' daily standup meeting. At The Commission, a change like this was so against the existing culture it simply fell flat on its face with many teams. However, this specific example was successful in a few circumstances. One team that was working on a large, multi-year HR system project had the executive sponsor attend two daily standup meetings each week. He was a strong supporter of the Kanban transformation and was completely bought into the process Having him attend the daily standup twice a week gave him insight into the reality of the project which allowed him to make decisions faster. Those decisions were based on reality, not a watered-down status report. Other executive sponsors had no interest in doing that and wanted to rely on status reports. **Side Note:** The responses of individual executive sponsors was a valuable Insight to us. We hadn't anticipated that, but we kept it in mind going forward. Keep your eyes and ears open for those kinds of Insights – they'll help you generate future Options!

- **Abandon:** These are Options that, after understanding the blast radius and sphere of influence, definitely won't work now, but might work later. The reason you keep them here is that you'll gain some Insights when other people see them and ask you about them. Putting those seemingly impossible ideas into people's brains might eventually morph them into "you know what, that's not such a bad idea!". Remember, just because you think it *won't* work, doesn't mean it *can't* work. At the Commission, we would review our Abandon list monthly and throw out any stale ideas. For example, removing performance bonuses that conflict with project priorities.

SHAPING YOUR CHANGE PLAN

By now your change plan should be taking shape. You've generated Insights, created Options, and have started thinking about how to sequence the changes you want to make. The difference with a Lean Change Management approach is that the plan will have come together more quickly because you've involved the people affected by these changes in the design of the changes. That may seem counter-intuitive to some of you. It means you've received feedback about the changes sooner which will help you make any necessary course corrections before spending too much time planning. At the very least, you've validated the plan with them *before* you implement it, and gotten their input and feedback on the changes.

Validating a change plan doesn't mean you've taken people away from their day job to sit with your change team for a week as you go through each step. It means you've brought them into the room and showed them your thought process, and the direction you're going. In a smaller organization, you could do that with everyone. In larger organizations, you may want to involve only a couple of early adopters from various departments who are affected by the change. Either way, you've given them a window into what's coming, and shown them that you, as a change agent, are supporting and facilitating the change, not pushing it on them. Remember the solution-focused-thinking idea of considering the future state? This approach involves the people affected in the design of that future state, after all, they are the people who have to live with the change day-in and day-out. They'll be more likely to be onboard with it if they have a say in designing how to accomplish it.

A colleague, Heather Stagl of Enclaria [2], once told me, *"If you're doing change management in your office with the door closed, you're doing it wrong."*

Wise words, and they closely align with the mantra of Lean Change Management, which is *co-creation of change*. People are more likely to support the change if they have input into the design of it, instead of having the change forced on them.

At this point, we've gone through a lot of theory, but haven't had any fun! Yes, the next part is what I call the fun part. Taking action. There is a chasm of difference between which changes we say we would implement, versus the ones we actually *do*.

In the next chapter, I'll show you how to leap off the edge of theory, and into the stormy waters of Experiments so you can learn how to introduce and manage change live, and *in action*!

7
EXPERIMENTS

CONTINUOUS CHANGE OVER BIG TRANSFORMATION

7. EXPERIMENTS

"Let's start all projects in the red, then move them to green status once we know they are on target" – I suggested.

"Um...well...uh...", was the worried reaction by Frank the PMO Director. Well, his actual reaction was stunned silence. I thought this description was better than starting off a chapter with a blank page, don't you agree? ☺ The CIO, on the other hand, loved the idea, but since Frank was the guy who would have to explain this to everyone, he decided to hold off on this Experiment.

The QMO continued to socialize the *start everything red* Experiment, but we never managed to try it at The Commission. In fact, I've tried to persuade other organizations I've worked with to start projects as red, but so far, I've got no takers! It seems these organizations are happy with the façade of certainty that green status reports provide.

I have learned through long and arduous experience that software teams discover risk early in the project, and have the most questions at this early stage. However, by the time the status report drives through the chain-of-command carwash, it's shiny, polished, and green. Uncertainty is at its highest at the start of the project, so start red and learn your way to green!

Cynicism aside, you're now ready to take action, so buckle up and hang on for the ride!

WHY EXPERIMENTS?

Can't we just call changes, *changes*? Referring to them as Experiments is deliberate. It's to get you, the change agent, thinking about the people who are affected by the change. Remember, the changes you're planning may seem simple and straightforward to you, but they might be confusing to the people affected by it.

At The Commission, and other organizations where I've worked, the change team spent a great deal of time thinking about changes. It is only natural that it should take the affected people just as much, if not more, time to reach the level of understanding the change team have about the change. In some of the projects I participated in, I spent so much time just *thinking* about a change that I was surprised the people affected by the change were not on board. I thought, "But it makes SO much sense! How can they NOT agree?" However their reaction was natural.

While *you*, the change agent, may feel more certainty about the change, it's still an Experiment because of the unpredictable reaction people will have to the change. You should also be aware that there might be unexpected impacts in areas of the organization you didn't previously consider. Calling changes "Experiments" helps you develop an approach that makes it ok to not know everything upfront.

It will also help you be more creative and learn while the change is in progress.

This change in mindset is helpful for change agents, and the people affected by the change, because it helps both feel better about the uncertainty that change brings.

CREATING HYPOTHESES FOR EXPERIMENTS

All Experiments start with a hypothesis. Early on at The Commission we were deliberate about creating hypotheses for *all* the changes we wanted to implement. After a while, we stopped creating hypotheses, except for changes that had a large blast radius or high uncertainty.

For example, let's use my favorite organizational victim, er, I mean, artifact, the status report. Some project managers at The Commission were creating weekly and monthly status reports for stakeholders, managers, and the PMO. Some stakeholders wanted more detail, some wanted less, and some didn't care because they didn't read them anyway.

Here's how I wrote down my hypothesis at the time:

> *I hypothesize that by changing our Enterprise Kanban Board (EKB) to be a portfolio-level board, we can eliminate weekly status reports PM's currently produce, thus reducing their administrative activities, which will save the department $150K annually, as measured by the time it takes 25 PMs to generate these reports.*

A colleague and I mocked up a "status-y looking" visualization on the Enterprise Kanban Board (EKB), leaving it intentionally rough-looking around the edges. The goal was to get feedback quickly, and not to have it perfect right from the start. Once we felt the visualization was good enough, we invited the PMO to have a look. I flat-out asked them, *"If we show you this data, can the weekly status reports go away?"*

Frank enthusiastically replied, *"YES!!"* The PMO was only concerned with satisfying a regulatory requirement with monthly status reports. The PMO was accountable for meeting this regulation through the monthly status reports that the PM's delivered to them. They would be happy to see weekly status reports eliminated because managing them was extra administrative work. Plus they admitted that most stakeholders didn't even look at them!

Since I had already established relationships with many people in the PMO, my gut told me this approach to ridding The Commission of weekly status reports would work. After this Experiment, the PMO communicated to the PM's that they did not want weekly status reports. If some PM's still wanted to produce them for their stakeholders, fine, but it wasn't a required artifact anymore.

The purpose of the EKB was starting to evolve. Originally, the external consultants owned it and changed it frequently. The intent was to help the people at The Commission understand the work better, but we observed that most people were confused by the frequent changes, and worse, they didn't feel they owned it.

We decided it was time for another Experiment!

The QMO took over the EKB, and we let it *die on the vine*, so to speak. That is, we stopped updating it, and the data posted in it became stale. Our hypothesis was that no matter how much we pushed, no one was going to use the EKB if they didn't own it. About two months later, one of the managers pointed to it and said, "You know guys, we could use this wall to visualize our work!" I nearly broke out into applause when I heard this!

While both the status report, and the *EKB ownership* Experiments were successful, not every Experiment worked out as we expected them to. Over time, you'll learn how your organization reacts to your Experiments. That will give you a good feel about what changes are more likely to be the right ones to implement.

After we learned which types of Experiments worked and which ones didn't at The Commission, it was much easier for us to not create hypotheses for our Experiments all the time. However, regardless if we actually created the hypotheses, we would always follow the same thought process:

• Think about what the Experiment would be
• Think about who would be affected
• Think about what the benefit would be
• Think about how to validate the Experiment as successful

HYPOTHESIS CREATION TEMPLATE

Here is a template you can use to create your hypotheses:

We hypothesize by <implementing this change>
we will <solve this problem>
which will have <these benefits>
as measured by <this measurement>

This template helps change agents get into the mindset of being explicit about Experiments. You'll get better at measuring your Experiments when you explicitly state the benefit, measurement and goal for them.

Another benefit is that the template uses plain language that everyone can understand, not change management "mumbo jumbo" that seems complicated.

Over time, this approach will feel much more natural to you, but in the beginning, be deliberate about writing a hypothesis using this template. Similar to learning how to use any new technique, deliberately practicing writing hypotheses will help you integrate that skill into your change toolkit.

VALIDATING EXPERIMENTS

While writing this chapter I started working with a new change team that had very little change management experience. To me, it seemed that every change they wanted to do resulted in the creation of a framework or 200-slide Powerpoint presentation about the new process they wanted to implement. The team would agree that they all loved *the deck* that had been created! During our team retrospective I brought up my observation that as a change team, we were too focused on checking-off change tasks as complete, instead of being focused on outcomes and validation. How could we validate if designing these new frameworks and processes were the right things to do?

More than half the team agreed...privately, of course. In the public retrospective, my observation was met with extreme pushback from the more vocal team members. Yet, after the retrospective, more than half the team emailed me privately to thank me for bringing it up because they were experiencing the same feeling.

To me, this team was more focused on how good *they* felt about the change, but hadn't considered what would happen when they tried to install that change into the organization.

"Validation" in Lean Change Management means confirming that the change you're planning is the right one to focus on for *that* particular time, before you spend all your time and effort designing a change that is likely to hit a wall of resistance. (Remember, resistance is the signal that tells you it's the wrong change for that particular time.)

Validating Experiments comes down to completing two important steps during the creation of your Experiment. The first step is done with your change team, and involves asking two questions before running the Experiment:

1. How will we know this Experiment has been successful?
2. How will know we are moving towards our intended outcome?

The second step is to review your Experiment with the people affected by the change to see how they react to it. If they react violently – metaphorically speaking – your Experiment might be a bad idea! Or it simply might not be the *right time* to introduce it.

In contrast, early on at The Commission, the validation of our Experiments happened *after* their introduction. More specifically, the external consultants were trying to measure the change in behaviors they expected to see when a change was introduced. They referred to it as "validated learning". I didn't agree with this approach, as I felt there were more important measures to focus on.

Measuring behavior can be dangerous. As soon as people feel they're being measured, they begin to feel threatened. This is a false feeling, and definitely not the intent, but nonetheless, that's usually what happens. The intent behind the behavior measurment was good, but the negative feelings it generated with the staff didn't help the change team gain trust and credibility.

There are more important things to measure than people's behavior:

- Did the people affected by the change get the outcome they thought they would?
- Has this Experiment improved something for them or made them happier?

For example, when organizations adopt Lean and Agile software practices, they expect teams to deliver higher quality software. That's the outcome, and it can be measured by a reduction of problems reported by customers. In order to deliver on that outcome, cross-functional teams consisting of developers, testers and business people, are created.

When we started our cross-functional team Experiment, we showed the team a collection of new Agile and Lean practices that they could implement in order to increase quality. This Experiment included talking with the team about a number of different practices they could use in order to produce higher quality software. Some of those practices were improved development and testing practices, and some were more about tweaking existing processes. All of the practices required the people on the team to behave differently.

Our validation for this Experiment focused on these outcomes:

- Implementation of better software practices leading to fewer defects as measured by in-process defects and escaped defects. The team tracked and categorized defects found in the team (in-process defects) and they tracked requests for changes requested from outside the team (escaped defects)

- A cross-functional team allowing the team to deliver their work sooner because there would be less time wasted on hand-offs between functional teams. For this validation, we used a simple, "softer" validation. We asked the team if they felt this was a more effective way to deliver software. They agreed it was, and told us why they felt that way. Some of those reasons ranged from shorter feedback loops to having people who didn't usually collaborate sit together.

Not every validation has to be, or can be, a scientific measurement. In the case of this Experiment, we used a mix of measurements to validate this type of change could work at The Commission.

One of the reasons I believe this Experiment worked is because we involved the team in the design of the change by giving them control over which practices they felt were achievable. I refer to this as "co-creation of change", because the people affected by the change are involved in the design of the change. They help decide what changes to implement, and how to validate that the Experiment worked.

As I workshopped the idea of co-creation of change with other organizations, two main points of opposition became clear:

1. **Big companies "can't" do this:** Well, that's what they all say. "Can't" actually means, "This approach won't work in our culture." It sounds good to "co-create change" but some people felt necessary structure was missing from this feedback-driven approach. The perceived lack of a plan up-front was unsettling for them.

2. **Project-focused approach:** All the larger organizations I worked with (10,000+ people) ran transformational change the same way they ran other projects: there is a budget, timeline, and scope. They know this approach is at odds with the dynamic and unpredictable nature of change, but they have to work within

those constraints largely because of how time is accounted for on the balance sheet. After all, *"That's how we've always done it"*.

THE FEEDBACK-DRIVEN APPROACH WORKS

Many organizations find the feedback-driven approach to be too *"fluffy"*. What's funny is that I found that experienced change agents who knew a lot about change methodologies were more likely to oppose the feedback-driven approach as it conflicted with what they've been doing their whole career. See that? Even change agents resist change!

On the flip side, people who were new to change management, or ones who were looking for more cutting-edge ideas about change methodologies LOVED the idea of a feedback-driven approach to change. The newbies had not yet become entrenched in the status quo of how organizations typically manage change through projects, schedules, and budgets.

The main concern the skeptics had with this *"fluffy"* approach was how they perceived and interpreted the phrase: *"feedback-driven approach to change"*. They simply heard *"go ask people what change we should work on"*, instead of what I really meant, which was, *"Use system feedback as input to your change plan."* They're not resistant to the approach itself, but simply the words used to describe it. Those words mess with their core beliefs. And that's ok.

Those who loved the idea of a feedback-driven approach to change were already starting with a different set of core beliefs. They were already *there*! They *got it*. If you find yourself thinking, *"Yes!! exactly!!"* while reading this book, welcome to my change world!

While skeptics and adopters seemed to differ on their reaction to a feedback-driven approach to change, there was a common practice from Lean Change Management they did agree on. They felt using big, visible planning tools – called canvases – helped them plan more effectively. Canvases are one-page templates used for planning everything from a straight change project to replacing a business case document. Don't worry if that term is foreign to you now, I'll show you some examples next.

PLANNING TOOLS: CANVASES

Alex Osterwalder popularized the idea of canvases in his book, *Business Model Generation*. His Business Model Canvas is one of the most popular planning tools, which eliminates the need for long, not-so-useful business cases, and is easily understood by everyone.

Some of you may have heard of the Business Model Canvas that emerged out of the Lean Startup community. Before it became all the rage, the A3 report was used extensively at Toyota. Taiichi Ohno, considered the father of the Toyota Production System, refused to read more than the first page of status reports! After he read the first page, he'd say *"Let's go see"*, which is often referred in Lean as *"Going to the Gemba"*. Taiichi Ohno wanted to see the real place of change, the workplace. Long (and mostly boring) reports were an impediment to real understanding, so he created the A3 report. The A3 report is another example of how simple, one-page documents can convey the most important information needed to act.

My first experience with using canvases comes from the book *Mastering the Rockefeller Habits* by Verne Harnish. Verne popularized a one-page strategic planning tool designed to help fast-growing organizations evolve their strategy into tactical plans, which helps leaders align their organizations.

Many years ago, before my Commission days, I worked for a fast-growing organization where the CEO bought a copy of this book for the leadership team, and after one read through, all of my confirmation bias sensors were screaming! The ideas in the book were so in line with my beliefs that I thought my hair was on fire! (And that was a good thing, believe me.) We used the one-page approach to plans for a year, and it helped the leadership team show the rest of the organization exactly where we were headed. The entire organization gained the clarity it needed to move forward.

THE FORMAT OF YOUR CANVAS MATTERS LESS THAN THE CONVERSATION THAT CREATES IT!

My point here is that plans don't need to be overly complex. The *act of planning* is the important part, not *the thing you develop (aka the plan)*. Using one-page planning tools are quick and efficient, and satisfies the need our brains have for certainty.

Here's how the QMO used various canvases to manage change at The Commission.

THE IMPROVEMENT CANVAS

We learned early on at The Commission that people and teams felt surprised by having our QMO coaches parachute into their team with a list of improvements. At that point, we were using the typical, traditional approach to change: plan the change behind closed doors and push it onto people.

One of the external consultants, Richard, had a great idea to solve this problem. He created a simple Kanban board on a flip chart, and posted it close to the team he was working with.

This board had a list of potential improvements in a To Do column. The team could see what improvements Richard was considering, which gave the team complete control over which ones to select from the list. We all loved the idea so we started doing it with our teams too.

Fellow QMO coach Bernadette Dario expanded on the Kanban board Richard used. She developed the Improvement Canvas, which was based on Lean, and inspired by the Improvement Kata created by Mike Rother, author of *Toyota Kata* [2]. Made up of four steps, the Improvement Kata is a practice built into Toyota's culture that has helped them make improvements part of everyday work.

Teams could pull their own improvements when they made sense.

This canvas works very well in support of incremental changes. It helps people understand where they are and where they are trying to get.

The four steps to the Improvement Kata are:
1. Understand the Direction
2. Grasp the Current Condition
3. Establish the Target Condition
4. PDCA (Plan, Do, Check, Act) towards the Target Condition

Below is the canvas that emerged at The Commission by applying those sequences:

Vision: What is the vision for the challenge we're trying to solve?

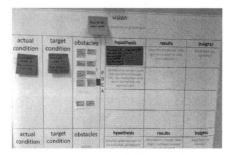

Visualize the details of Experiments.

Actual Condition: What is the current state?

Target Condition: What is the future state?

Obstacles: What would prevent us from achieving the Target Conditions?

Hypothesis: What's our specific hypothesis for the change?

Results: What were the actual results?

Insights: What Insights emerged while working on this improvement?

USING THE ONE-PAGE CHANGE PLAN

The Improvement Canvas works extremely well when uncertainty is fairly low. This One-Page Change Plan is more helpful when uncertainty is high because you may not know exactly what you want your future state to be.

1. **Problem Statement:** What problem are we trying to solve?

2. **Options:** What Options do we have to solve this problem?

ONE PAGE CHANGE PLAN

WHAT PROBLEM ARE WE TRYING TO SOLVE?

WHAT OPTIONS ARE YOU TRYING TO SOLVE?

WHAT OPTIONS DO WE HAVE?

LIST 3 SOLUTIONS

WHAT ARE THE RISKS FOR EACH SOLUTION?

LIST RISKS ASSOCIATED WITH EACH SOLUTION

WHAT DO WE NEED TO DO?

TO DO	IP	DONE

HOW WILL WE MEASURE PROGRESS?

WHAT METRICS WILL YOU USE TO MEASURE PROGRESS?

INSIGHTS

WHAT IS WORKING, WHAT ISN'T WORKING.

Answers the who, what, why, when and how of change.

3. **Risks/Obstacles:** What are the risks and obstacles for each Option?

4. **Actions:** A simple Kanban board of actions we need to take in order to solve the problem.

5. **Measurements:** How will we show progress? How will we measure success?

6. **Insights:** What worked? What didn't?

Once created, post this canvas in a high-traffic area. Then tape a marker and some sticky notes to the wall beside it to encourage staff to post feedback in the Insights column.

Encouraging Feedback

In the beginning, you probably won't get any feedback, depending on how unusual this approach is for your culture. To solve that, organize some Lean Coffee sessions to socialize the canvas and specifically ask for feedback.

If your organization loves its Powerpoint presentations for everything, then create a slide that shows this canvas *and* bring a physical copy of the canvas with you to the next change meeting. That's an Experiment in and of itself!

Some people may love the idea of posting the canvas in an open area where people can see it and comment on it. Conversely, some might be scared to death to try that! Knowing who likes visibility and who is scared by it is an important Insight to use in your planning.

Back at The Commission...

I always used the physical canvas, because I wanted people to get out of their seats at meetings and become physically involved in the process through the use of sticky notes. I found the physical action of writing sticky notes and moving them around helped people be more involved in the change. Does this approach work in more traditional companies? I'll bet you were going to say no, right? Well, you'd be wrong! In fact, here are a couple of quotes from the organizational effectiveness group at a Fortune 100 company I worked with:

> *"I love it! [the canvas], using sticky notes, and seeing
> a quick glance of the activities that are happening is fantastic!
> It's easy to move stickies, it's visual, and easy to change"*

> *"I like that it's more of a conversation and less of a
> heavy duty change plan, it still documents things and
> keeps people aligned"*

If people in a 100,000+ person organization think light-weight planning tools work, I'm sure it'll work for you!

And these are only two examples of canvases I've used. Find more at http://leanchange.org/canvases

If the concept of using canvases is new to you, try the Improvement Canvas or the One-Page Change Plan canvas first. Over time, you'll be able to experiment with your own canvases and customize them to suit your needs. Remember, the shared understanding that happens as a result of the conversation is more important than what particular canvas you use. The hardest part about using canvases is figuring out what measurements to use in order to show progress towards the change.

MEASURING EXPERIMENTS

What I takeaway from that quote is: Be careful about how you measure progress because it'll influence behavior. Remember how I talked about that a little earlier? About how measuring behaviour can be dangerous? Well, here's why.

> # WHAT GETS MEASURED GETS MANAGED
> - PETER DRUCKER -
> MANAGEMENT GURU

I once worked in an organization that prided itself on having high employee engagement scores. The problem was, employees were incentivized to fill out those engagement scores via performance reviews. So the organization got exactly what they wanted: High engagement scores! Unfortunately, those numbers didn't tell the true story: a large portion of the staff was miserable, and HR flat-out told me their engagement score was "S-<redacted>", ahem, insert your favorite colorful word here!

At The Commission, we used a mix of qualitative, quantitative, leading, and lagging indicators to measure progress and outcomes. We wanted to measure the tangible business outcomes that organizations typically see when adopting Agile and Lean practices, but also intangible measures like, whether or not people feel that this way of working is more effective. That's important because the organization should be making progress towards their objectives, and people should be happier!

Qualitative Measures

At The Commission, we had 15-minute stand-up meetings in front of the Enterprise Kanban Board (EKB) to raise and resolve project risks and issues. As a coach, I didn't feel these were as effective as they could be, so I posted a poll asking for feedback. On the right side of the paper I wrote, *"This meeting is awesome!"* and on the other side, *"This meeting is terrible"*.

People voted by marking an "X" under the choice that reflected their opinion about them. Out of the roughly 30 people who regularly attended the meetings, only three people responded. So I dropped my pursuit of solving this problem. I considered this a qualitative measure because I was relying on feedback from meeting attendees about how they felt about the meeting, which is purely subjective. Apparently I was the only one who felt the meetings weren't effective, and the attendees didn't see it the same way. Had more people participated, I would have used those Insights as data for the next retrospective about how we could improve the meeting.

Quantitative Measures

We used surveys to collect hard data that would help us determine the next course of action to take, or changes to recommend. A popular measure we used was Net Promotor Score (NPS) [1]. Briefly, NPS is the answer to the question, "On a scale of 1 to 10, how likely would you recommend this product?" Promoters are those who vote 9 or 10, and detractors are those who vote 1 to 6; throw out any 7 and 8 votes.

To calculate NPS, subtract the percentage of detractors from the percentage of promoters. You'll end up with a score between -100 and +100, and that's your NPS.

SEPARATE MEASUREMENTS FROM DIAGNOSTICS

Here's the NPS question we used:

*"How likely would you recommend your
delivery team to another business unit?"*

The reasons we used this measurement were because the team had
no control over the results. The business stakeholders would either
recommend the team or they wouldn't. If they did, *yay team*! If
not, the results would provoke a conversation to find out why not.
Sometimes I find organizations only want to measure defects, and I
always advocate against doing that. Reason being, it's easily gamed
by the team. If you want defects to be reduced, they will be reduced
because the team may unintentionally label defects as 'features'.
Voila! Problem solved!

Leading Indicators

These measurements are helpful for showing progress towards a goal.
We used a measurement called the Happiness Index, which might
sound too touchy-feely, but stay with me here. A happier, less stressed
team delivers higher quality work. Don't believe me? Well, read the
book *Product-Focused Software Improvement* [3]. A study found in

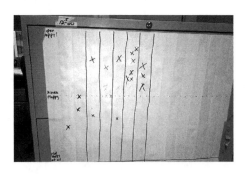

the book showed this exact
thing: happier employees are
less stressed, and therefore
produce higher quality work.
At The Commission, we saw a
dramatic increase in happiness
from the Architecture team
as measured by their team
happiness index they posted
on the wall.

Happier people are more productive!

We observed an increase in energy from the Architecture team, and more willingness on their part to prove they were a supporting function, not a controlling one. They started by doing an Architecture roadshow to help people understand what their responsibilities were and what help they could provide.

They also started hosting monthly architecture sessions to share information about the overall 3-year modernization program, which was more effective than the old way of adding documents to the internal Sharepoint site.

The Happiness Index chart itself wasn't the reason we saw this change in behavior. It was simply the trigger for the conversations between the Architecture team and their manager.

Another leading indicator we used to measure the overall software quality was in-process defects. In-process defects are problems found by the team within their development cycle. When the team measured the number of defects they produced before a production release, and that number declined over time, we can expect the lagging indicator of support calls will also decrease. So the *leading* indicator of less in-process defects, leads to the *lagging* indicator of less external defects, or support calls.

It is easy to find a number of Leading Indicators when it comes to measuring the development of software programs. But what about for measuring change? We used attendance to the Lean Coffee sessions and study group as leading indicators for adoption of the changes we were introducing. If attendance numbers remained relatively stable, we expected to see changes in behavior over time, because people were interested in learning about, and applying, new practices for managing work.

One example of the proof was when a team told us a story about how they were able to change the approach their business stakeholders took to signing off on requirements. Many team members on this project attended Lean Coffee sessions, study groups, and lunch and learn sessions.

They worked hard applying the new practices we were introducing, and after a number of months, their business partners stopped being rigid about sign-off. In fact, one of the Business Analysts said, *"Before this project, I've never before heard a business partner say 'we trust you, we have seen what you deliver in the past'"*.

Lagging Indicators

These measure change outcomes, and are much easier to identify than leading indicators. The challenge with lagging indicators is to avoid tying performance reviews and bonuses to them!

Use lagging indicators to validate your Experiments, and not as binary success and failure metrics that typically punish the people responsible for them. At The Commission, lagging indicators included:

Project Metrics
- Fewer escaped defects as a result of the adoption of the Agile and Lean practices we were introducing.
- Increased Net Promotor Score as a result of the more collaborative approach to executing projects.

Team Self-Assessments
- Adoption rate of Agile and Lean practices as measured by the team continually assessing how they were doing.
- Gut feel from the team that they were benefiting from these practices.

One of the teams at The Commission did an NPS with their business partners, and the result was zero. That didn't make them feel very good, because usually a zero is a bad thing, right? They'd forgotten that zero in the NPS world is right in the middle. They had just as many promoters as detractors. A bit later, after the next survey, their score increased into the positive numbers, as they had no detractors. They were happy about that!

Customer satisfaction, as measured by the lagging indicator of NPS, is the ultimate measure of success in my books. It proves the team is setting and delivering on the expectations of their customers, either internal or external to the organization. Using a mix of project metrics and team self-assessments also provided the teams powerful Insights into what they could improve next.

TEAM-DEFINED MEASUREMENTS

Organizations that subscribed to traditional management views tend to use top-down measurements overall, and performance reviews to make sure people align to achieving those outcomes.

To me, this is backward. The people doing the work are best able to define measurements at a tactical level. In order to define measurements that matter, management sets the context and strategic objective, and staff comes up with how they will measure themselves.

I attended a Franklin Covey seminar a few years ago, and the facilitator told a story about how one of their clients, a large resort, wanted to improve overall customer satisfaction scores. In short, management decided on an overall strategy and measurement, namely the overall customer satisfaction number, but allowed each department to define their own leading and lagging indicators.

For example, after many experiments, the valet group decided that a car retrieval time of zero was their leading indicator that would improve the lagging indicator of overall customer satisfaction. All the other groups provided their own measurements and over the span of a couple of years, the resort increased their overall customer satisfaction number from 52% to 68%.

Allowing teams to provide evidence they are aligning with your overall change strategy is more important than pushing measurements on them. It motivates the team to contribute because they'll feel a sense of ownership about their involvement in the change. The change sponsors will also benefit by getting better insights into how the change is progressing through feedback about the organizational reality from the people who do the actual work, every day.

This, along with co-creation of change, provides evidence of progress and shows you success takes work. A lot of work. That said, as a change agent, it's an unbelievable feeling to have someone thank me for helping them through a change instead of forcing them to comply with it. That's why I do what I do for a living.

In order for this approach to work, there must be strong alignment between executives, management, and staff. In the next chapter, I'll show you how to develop and achieve that alignment.

8
CREATING
ALIGNMENT
FOR CHANGE

CANVASES, VISUALIZATION AND CONVERSATIONS

8. CREATING ALIGNMENT FOR CHANGE

"I love the canvas, it's more of a conversation tool, less about creating heavy duty change plans, and it still documents things and keeps people aligned."

This quote is from Barb Heller, who is an Organizational Effectiveness Consultant at a Fortune 100 company, and someone who participated in a study group about the first edition of this book. We talked about how to apply ideas from Lean Change Management, specifically about how to satisfy stakeholders' needs to see change plans by using change canvases.

Change plans don't need to be big, heavy documents – in fact, they probably shouldn't be. After all, our brains like the certainty that comes through the *act of planning* not necessarily *the plan* itself. In his 2008 *Neuroleadership Journal* [1] whitepaper, David Rock notes that the act of breaking down a complex project into smaller, more manageable pieces satisfies the need our brains have for certainty.

Throughout my research for this book, which included attending numerous change management conferences, and talking to people in the traditional change management world, I noticed a strong bias towards the *big-plan-upfront* approach to change. Stakeholders wanted assurance that *the plan* would work, so naturally, change practitioners feel more pressure to spend time planning and documenting risks.

However, the Agile community's stance on change is that we must *embrace uncertainty* – we *can't* know everything upfront, and we need to accept that! We must **be** Agile, and use the values and principles of Agile to guide change.

That's a scary proposition for change practitioners and leaders who sometimes have their performance review, or more, tied to the successful implementation of a change.

Surely there must be a happy medium here.

I started my journey into exploring feedback-driven approaches to change by considering these questions:

1. Was it really *the plan* traditional change practitioners wanted?

2. Were they really just looking for a better way to *create alignment* within their organization to get people on board with the change?

I assumed the latter, so I began writing and speaking about why change methods and tools need to take a backseat to change facilitation and co-creation of change. Change is just as much an art as it is a science, but it seemed to me that too many people were focused on tools and methods. They weren't thinking of the art that's needed as well. As I presented ideas from this book at conferences, and held study groups on the first edition of this book, two problems became clear:

1. How can change practitioners convince stakeholders who sponsor change initiatives to accept the uncertainty that change brings, and use a feedback-driven approach to change instead of a solely plan-based approach?

2. How do change practitioners start a change initiative using the non-linear approach that Lean Change Management brings? That is, how can they plan without generating Insights? How long should they work on generation Insights before coming up with Options? How do they show change sponsors progress in times of high uncertainty?

After an 8-week study group session with Barb and the other organizational effectiveness practitioners at a Fortune 100 company was complete, we came to the following conclusions:

1. Change managers and organizational development people *know* that a feedback-driven approach to change is more effective. They also admit that all the upfront planning is helpful, but *the plan* doesn't survive first contact with the people affected by the change.

2. Creating alignment with lighter-weight planning tools is the key for convincing stakeholders that a plan is in place. The difference is that the plan is created through organizational feedback, as well as the observations and expertise of the change team.

3. Using some specific Agile practices, like retrospectives and lean coffee sessions, can dramatical reduce the symptom of resistance by creating an extra feedback loop about the change.

4. Visualizing the change through canvases and big information radiators are much more effective than traditional communication plans and software-based tools (*cough* SharePoint).

Overall, we determined there was an approach to gaining the certainty our brains need, with respect to the change plan, while accepting the uncertainty of change. Sounds a bit like magic doesn't it?

Well, it's not.

It's about combining all the ideas I've written about so far, and developing your own change process that is best suited to your organization. There are four components to developing your own change management process:

1. Develop your Strategic Change Canvas
2. Align Your Organization
3. Develop your Change Agent Network
4. Execute the Lean Change Management Cycle

Notice I refer to these as components, not steps. Your strategy will evolve as you learn. Your change agent network will evolve as more people align to the change. Your organizational alignment will vary as your change progresses.

All set? Let's dive into the details!

DEVELOP YOUR STRATEGIC CHANGE CANVAS

Starting with a change strategy isn't a new idea. The difference with this approach, however, is *how* you create it. You create it through a well-facilitated session using big, visible canvases, and sticky notes on a wall.

The canvas helps align people in your organization because it answers the important questions they have when change is introduced:

1. **What is the vision for our organization with respect to this change?**
   Remember the QMO's lighthouse? That was our vision, communicated as a picture. Once you've talked about the vision, it's a good idea to do a visioning exercise and create this metaphor or picture.

2. **Why is this change important to the organization?**
   This is Kotter's first step, Create Urgency. However, asking "Uh, what's the urgency?" is less effective than asking, "Why is this change important?" Remember, urgency is a matter of perspective, so consider multiple points of view while discussing this question.

3. **How will we measure success?**
   These are business objectives, typically lagging indicators.

4. **How will we show progress?**
   These are the leading indicators that show your organization is headed in the right direction. Quick Wins (Kotter's 6th step) are important to develop and maintain momentum with the change.

STRATEGIC CHANGE CANVAS

VISION	IMPORTANCE
WHAT IS THE VISION FOR THIS CHANGE?	WHY IS THIS CHANGE IMPORTANT TO OUR ORGANIZATION?

SUCCESS MEASUREMENTS	PROGRESS MEASUREMENTS
HOW WILL WE MEASURE SUCCESS?	HOW WILL WE SHOW PROGRESS TOWARDS OUR VISION?

WHO AND WHAT IS AFFECTED?

WHAT PEOPLE, DEPARTMENTS AND PROCESSES NEED TO CHANGE IN ORDER TO REALIZE OUR VISION?

HOW WILL WE SUPPORT PEOPLE?

WHAT ACTIONS WILL WE (THE CHANGE SPONSORS AND CHANGE TEAM) DO TO SUPPORT PEOPLE THROUGH THE CHANGE?

WHAT IS OUR PLAN?	-1 MONTH	NEXT	PREPARE	INTRODUCE	REVIEW
OPTIONS: A LIST OF POSSIBLE EXPERIMENTS	EXPERIMENTS LIKELY TO BE INTRODUCED IN ABOUT A MONTH	THE NEXT MOST IMPORTANT CHANGES TO INTRODUCE	EXPERIMENTS BEING PLANNED AND VALIDATED	EXPERIMENTS IN PROGRESS	EXPERIMENTS BEING REVIEWED

Use it 'as-is' or customize to suit your needs.

5. **Who is affected by the change and what will they need to do differently?**

You can explore this question using the McKinsey 7S model. Consider the blast radius of the change and how a change to strategy will impact the other 6 dimensions in the McKinsey model.

6. **How will the change team support people through the transition?**

This is your support and communication plan. How will you communicate the change? Collect feedback about the change?

7. **What's our plan?**

This section uses ideas from Kanban to help you sequence the changes. Which changes are the best to start with? Which ones should wait? Which changes are far too big to tackle right now? One of the principles of Kanban is to limit work in progress. Limiting the number of changes in progress will reduce the change fatigue effect.

Facilitating a Strategic Change Canvas Session

There are plenty of approaches for group facilitation. I'm sure your favourite search engine can help you find a whole bunch! Regardless of the approach you take, the most important thing to do is to visualize the canvas on a wall using sticky notes.

If you're really stuck and don't have access to a skilled facilitator, simply buy everyone a copy of this book, have them read it for homework, and then go through the seven questions above one by one!

Seriously though, those seven steps are a great place to start because they answer the most important questions about the change. Sometimes when embarking on using a new technique, following a guide is a great place to start. Try this approach and then customize it later.

Once you have a Strategic Change Canvas in place, it's a good idea to get a good night's sleep and review it the next day.

After a quick refresher, use these questions as a guide to complete your Strategic Change Canvas 1.0:

1. What points haven't we considered yet?
2. What are our assumptions about this strategy?
3. What is our riskiest assumption?
4. How often should we review this strategy?
5. How will we collect feedback from staff?
6. What other important information should we put on this canvas?

Oh, and you see the version number I put in the canvas name? I did that on purpose. This is a living artifact, not a one-and-done artifact. That means it'll evolve as you learn, and it's a good, visual signal to people that something has changed when they see a new version number on the physical canvas.

Who Should Be Involved:

The change sponsor: This could be a C-Level executive, or VP.

The change team: This is the team, employees or consultants, that will facilitate the change. HINT: It's a really good idea to not solely rely on consultants here!

The executive team (Optional): Depending on the size and structure of your organization, you may limit attendance at this Strategic Change Canvas creation session. Use your best judgement!

Once the Strategic Change Canvas has been created, it's time to start aligning people in your organization with your change strategy.

ALIGN YOUR ORGANIZATION

Depending on the size of your organization, and the type of change you're implementing, this can be a ton of work!

At The Commission, the external consultants hosted a 2-day Kanban workshop which essentially was the kickoff of the Kanban transformation. It was more training than alignment, so there wasn't a lot of "why we are doing this" conversations, but nonetheless, everybody knew what the change was.

There are many approaches you can take to aligning people around the change you're implementing, but the objective is to validate the Strategic Change Canvas and collect Insights from everyone who is affected.

If your organization is relatively small, say, less than a couple hundred people, you can facilitate a session with everyone, including management and staff. At Barb's organization, we facilitated a session with 150 people who were part of the leadership development program. It takes some planning, but it's doable. Again, search online and I'm sure you'll find a whole bunch – I can't tell you everything, right? ☺

That said, here are a couple of quick pointers that will help:

1. In larger organizations, re-purpose an existing department meeting and have the manager and a member of the change team present the Strategic Change Canvas.

2. In smaller organizations, bring in lunch and do a full-day all-company session using one of the large group facilitation approaches you searched online!

3. As-needed-basis: Facilitate this session starting with the first people, departments, or teams that are affected by the change.

4. Administer an ADKAR® Assessment Survey.

If you skipped over it for some reason, have a peek at Chapter 4 where I described how we used an ADKAR® survey at The Commission. At a different organization that was embarking on a 3-year Agile transformation program, we didn't use the ADKAR® assessment, but instead we:

1. Created the Strategic Change Canvas with the VP leadership team, which consisted of six people.

2. Aligned the change team based on the output of the first session. At the time, the change team consisted of about 20 people.

3. Aligned the teams affected by the change when new teams were created.

4. Collected Insights during monthly all-team retrospectives and weekly Lean Coffee sessions.

This happened over the course of five months. Early on, the feedback was overwhelmingly negative. We heard comments like *"This will never work here!!!"* but over time and through reinforcement, people started to get onboard with the changes.

Keep Your Eyes Open!

However you choose to facilitate sessions to align people in the organization around the Strategic Change Canvas, keep your eyes open! Write down your observations while this session is going on. You'll notice that some people will immediately align with the strategy, and those people will likely become your early adopters. You can recruit these people to be part of your change agent network!

Tactical Change Canvases

At The Commission, teams were able to pull the changes they could absorb into the regular work stream. The Improvement Canvases from Chapter 7 were perfect for this approach. For larger changes, and larger organizations, create a higher-level team or department canvas.

These are the important questions to ask in order to create a team or department level canvas:

- What people, departments and/or processes in our organization is supporting this change?
- What in our organization would work against this change?
- How can our team or department contribute to this strategy?
- What help do we need to execute this strategy?

This exercise kicks off the alignment process. Teams and/or departments can start adding Experiments on their tactical canvas and, if need be, dive deeper into the Experiments by using Improvement Canvases. Similar to the Strategic Change Canvas, this Tactical Canvas needs to be made visible.

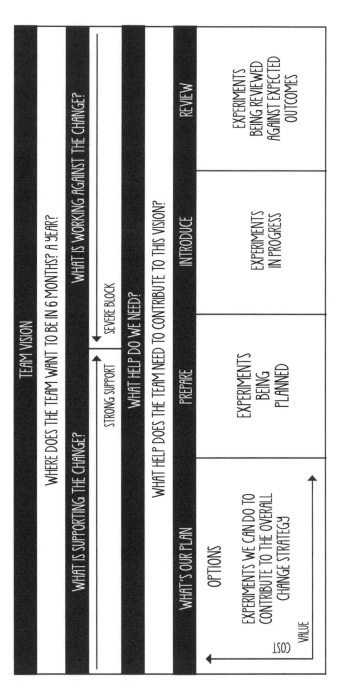

TEAM / DEPARTMENT CHANGE CANVAS

TEAM VISION

WHERE DOES THE TEAM WANT TO BE IN 6 MONTHS? A YEAR?

WHAT IS SUPPORTING THE CHANGE?   WHAT IS WORKING AGAINST THE CHANGE?

STRONG SUPPORT   SEVERE BLOCK

WHAT HELP DO WE NEED?

WHAT HELP DOES THE TEAM NEED TO CONTRIBUTE TO THIS VISION?

WHAT'S OUR PLAN	PREPARE	INTRODUCE	REVIEW
OPTIONS			
EXPERIMENTS WE CAN DO TO CONTRIBUTE TO THE OVERALL CHANGE STRATEGY	EXPERIMENTS BEING PLANNED	EXPERIMENTS IN PROGRESS	EXPERIMENTS BEING REVIEWED AGAINST EXPECTED OUTCOMES

VALUE

COST

Let teams and departments own their changes that align with your strategy.

For the executives and change sponsors, be more concerned that teams and departments are providing evidence that they're aligning to the change, but leave the details to the teams. That includes measurements, so resist the urge to tell people how you'll measure them, and let them figure out their own progress measurements.

Again, creating organizational alignment around a change is extremely difficult and time consuming, especially in larger organizations. Be patient!

DEVELOP YOUR CHANGE AGENT NETWORK

It's possible you have a dedicated change management team, or at least somebody who's responsible for implementing the change from the side of their desk. Regardless of who it is, they'll need help!

You will need executives, managers, and staff to act as change agents. That's because people are more likely to listen to, and work with, their peers rather than external consultants or dedicated change managers. People tend to feel threatened or feel that change is being pushed on them if they don't see their peers jumping in first. This approach helps the change go viral, and helps build momentum.

Here are some tips for expanding your change team:
- Get at least one person from each department that is affected by the change.

- Set strong expectations with the early adopters that being part of the change team is extra work.

- Make becoming a member of the change agent network exclusive in order to attract the right people. I've always wanted to try some

American Idol style audition, but that has been too crazy of an idea for the organizations I've worked in!

- Agree on rotating the change team members periodically, depending on the type of change you're implementing.

Most of all, give these early adopters support, training, and some autonomy. Notice I said some autonomy. At this point you want the people who are motivated to help execute the change, but be aware, they may not have the necessary skills you, as a change agent, have.

Remember, at The Commission, we didn't do a stellar job of recruiting people to become part of the change team. At a different organization, our change team did this extremely well. We hosted weekly lean coffee sessions and monthly retrospectives designed to build alignment and generate feedback about the change, and slowly, people outside the core change team started showing interest in helping.

CHANGE GOES VIRAL WHEN PEOPLE START HELPING OTHER PEOPLE ADJUST

These people, who weren't part of the core change team, starting taking ownership of roadblocks all the teams were facing. They would provide updates to the whole department during our monthly retrospectives and the change team supported their efforts.

Over time, the change team started backing away from facilitating these retrospective sessions, and encouraged people on teams to tell their stories to others.

Another tactic we used to help build the change happened organically, during new team kickoff meetings. We would invite team members from other teams who had been through the same change to talk about their experience. We encouraged them to be completely open and honest about their experiences.

I had started working with a new team and invited a couple of people from a team who had been through this change a few months earlier. I'll never forget how they described the experience. They said the change really sucked for a while! They also said their consultant was full of *beep*, and they were stressed for a couple of months as they fought through the change.

Then, they said, little by little, things got better. They realized their consultant was there to help them, and that they had to learn to work together as a team. Now they wouldn't go back to the old way of working because the new way was so much better! That was both refreshing and scary for the new team I was working with.

This is why developing your Change Agent Network is important. You can have an official Change Agent Network that is supported by the organization, or you can go the organic route. Or both!

The point is, the employees of the company from the top, all the way down, need to own the change.

EXECUTE THE LEAN CHANGE MANAGEMENT CYCLE

Creating a strategy, alignment, and a change team aren't new ideas. Any change program that wants a chance to succeed needs these basic building blocks.

The Onirik study I cited in Chapter 1 mentioned that the lack of a structured change process is why change "fails". Change fails when the people managing the change blindly follow a structured process that isn't compatible with the organization.

This is why you need to build your own change management process, using the Lean Change Management cycle. Here's how to do it:

1. **Create a change program room:** Make your plan visible, that includes your Strategic Change Canvas and Experiments.

2. **Decide how often to have these meetings:**
    *   **Change Team Daily Standups:** Yes, it's called a *daily* standup, which is a practice taken from the Scrum methodology, but you don't actually have to have it daily. Meet for 15-minutes on a regular schedule depending on how chaotic your change is. At The Commission, we started with dailies, and as we became busy, we reduced it to twice a week.
    *   **Change Team Retrospectives:** This meeting is for the change team to tweak their change management process and figure out how to work more effectively as a team. At The Commission, we did this monthly.
    *   **Strategic Change Canvas Refresh:** This meeting is for revising the Strategic Change Canvas based on how the change is unfolding. I usually recommend doing this quarterly, but at The Commission, we did it when it was necessary. That was usually due to an un-expected event, like when the external consultants left, and when their was a major organizational change that was triggered from somewhere else in the organization.
    *   **Lean Coffee** [2]**:** This meeting is to continually reinforce alignment and collect feedback from people affected by the change. At The Commission, we did this weekly. At a different

organization, we had a face-to-face lean coffee every other week, and a completely virtual sessions on the off-week.

- **Retrospectives:** This meeting is to collect Insights about the tactical changes that are in progress. At The Commission, we did team and department retrospectives, and combined the data later. At a different organization, we held monthly retrospectives which were open to everyone affected by the change.

3. **Status Reporting:** First off, STOP USING STATUS REPORTS! Yes, this will be tough, but it's supposed to be hard. Get change sponsors, executives, and people affected by the change into a big, visible room...you know, the one you created in Step 1. I recommend not backing down easily from this one. It will be painful, but worth it. Remember, urgency for change happens when open and honest dialogue happens, and we all know how "honest" the data on the status report is.

These three pieces are the core ingredients you need in order to build your own change process. The details will emerge over time as you learn how your organization reacts to change. Avoid creating on too much process at the beginning, stay lean!

The interactions between your change sponsors, executives, change team, and people affected by the change will be better equipped to deal with the complexity. Create only enough process in order to trigger these interactions.

But wait, what about a communication plan? Communication happens during these interactions, right? Depending on the type

A DOCUMENTED, DETAILED PROCESS CANNOT MATCH THE COMPLEXITY OF THE HUMAN BRAIN!

of change you're implementing, you will need to generate official communications. Resist the desire to build a SharePoint site, create a newsletter, and start an email campaign. Do as much as you can organically – within reason of course.

As you execute your change using Lean Change Management [3], remember these two guiding principles:

1. You cannot control how people will respond to change when it's introduced.
2. People are more likely to support a change when they have input into its design.

SO, WHAT HAPPENED AT THE COMMISSION?

I've shown many examples about the incremental improvements we made at The Commission. But was the change successful, or is it part of that dreadful, and wrong, 70% failure stat?

Well, that depends...

WHAT WORKED VERY WELL HERE

- Using canvases to communicate change and improvement initiatives.

- Allowing teams to *pull* improvements rather than force change on them.

- The QMO team was the best group of change agents I've ever worked with.

- Big visible information radiators.

- Lean coffee sessions to promote open dialogue.

- Dedication from the staff to learn new ways of managing work.

- Our dedication to following the Lean Change Management Cycle eventually became the way we worked. We were less deliberate about "following the process", and found a rhythm that worked better for us.

WHAT WE COULD HAVE IMPROVED

- Be more clear that we needed more executive and management buy-in.

- Involved more employees in the change team.

- Have a better understanding of the level of disruption that was tolerable by the organization.

- Moved to a cross-functional team approach sooner instead of trying to get functional groups to handoff work to each other more effectively.

- Re-invented our approach to change less often so we didn't confuse people.

As of the release date of this book, The Commission was two years into their 3-year transformation, and their focus has shifted away from transformation, and more towards process improvement.

After the first year of "the Kanban transformation", the change project was considered to be *done*, and the QMO went into process improvement and support mode. After a year, half of the QMO team members moved on to other organizations, but the remaining team members still possess strong Agile and Lean skills, so they are continuing to see benefits from the adoption of new processes.

To reiterate my question, would I consider this change initiative to sit in the 70% failure bucket, or 30% success bucket?

Well, it's not that simple. We experienced many successes, including motivating some of the early adopters to find jobs in other organizations! That's a success for me, and something I typically see when organizations bring in Agile practices. The early adopters love these ideas, and when they feel the organization isn't supporting the wide-spread adoption of them, they leave for another organization where they can use these practices.

That makes them happy, and I consider that a win.

I also consider the visibility and co-ordination of the 3-year modernization program to be a success because it helped people co-ordinate work more effectively. The program itself will get done, and I saw enough evidence to lead me to the conclusion that the practices we implemented during the Kanban transformation helped people make sense of an incredibly complex modernization program.

Overall, I feel that the Kanban transformation brought meaningful change into the lives of many people at The Commission, and that is what is important to me. Not only did the people affected by the change benefit by learning new practices for building software, so did I. I learned a great deal about change from my fellow QMO'ers and also from the external consultants.

CREDITS, TIDBITS
AND REFERENCES

CREDITS, TIDBITS AND REFERENCES

It is a warm, beautiful, and sunny day here in Munich, Germany as I finish the final chapter! Today I was fortunate to have Torsten Scheller (www.leanchange.de), friend and Godfather backer of the Happy Melly crowd funding campaign, give me a tour of beautiful downtown Munich.

I couldn't have imagined an ending such as this when I hit *Publish* on the first chapter of the first edition of this book back in 2012. Nor could I have envisioned the road I was embarking on when I first began writing more about organizational change, and less about Agile back in 2009. Years of experiments, connecting with people, visualizing one-page change plans, and a whole lot of free consulting has finally brought me here, to Munich.

A week where I finished this book and delivered the first two Lean Change Management workshops (www.leanchange.org/workshop).

I learned that Germans like their structure and process, but despite the cultural differences between Germans and Canadians, our challenges with changes are the same. I can summarize that with one of my favourite quotes from Gerry Weinberg:

"Whatever the problem, it's always a people problem"

I suspect this is true, regardless of cultural background!

This book would not have been possible without a great deal of help from some incredibly talented people. I'm sure I'll forget someone who contributed either through feedback, direct help and support, or plain old conversations, so in true Canadian fashion, I will apologize for that now!

(By the way, you can send Kudos to anyone at www.kudobox.co)

KUDOS!

While I could write pages upon pages of thank you notes, I will give extra thanks to those who directly contributed to this journey.

My Family

Christine, Owen, and Abby, my beloved family. Yes, family comes first, but sometimes mine came second as I missed deadlines for this book, worked with multiple clients, developed a college course, ran workshops, and fell asleep on the couch, instead of giving them the love and attention they deserved.

They endured my grumpiness, mood swings, and frustrations for months while my brain struggled with the mind-numbing attention to detail required by a book. It wasn't constant chaos at our house, as we did make time for small vacations here and there, and I truly thank all of you for putting up with me!

Happy Melly Express

To Vasco Duarte and Lisette Sutherland, my core team members, rockstars, and disciplinarians!

Vasco, I don't know how many times you heard me say, or email, "Yeah, I'll finish that by tomorrow" only to take an extra few days (or weeks) to finish whatever it was! You kept me on top of what I needed to do, and kicked my butt when needed. You challenged my assumptions, gave me brutal truth feedback during the editing process, and wore funny decorations during our Google Hangout calls. Thank you, you rock!

Lisette, you helped me reach a new level of awesomeness with your ninja-like marketing skills, and warm and funny demeanour! Thank you for all the help with the social campaigns, getting podcasts organized, marketing ideas, and blog posts. The hours of research and work, especially with the social media support, was invaluable to me, thank you!

Jurgen Appelo

To my writing coach! I was honoured to have the Feedback Wrap tested on me! Not only was that more effective for giving feedback, but your actual feedback helped me improve my confidence when I was feeling like everything I was writing was utter crap!

It's been inspiring to hear your feedback, and pair-train with you. Thank you for all your help and inspirational ideas!

Agil Werden and Torsten Scheller
www.agil-werden.de

My friend, Godfather backer, and fellow introvert! Thank you for inviting me into your home in Munich and for organizing the first Lean Change Management workshops! I appreciate how much time you spent helping organize the material, and most importantly, for pushing me into trying a new facilitation style for the workshop. If it wasn't for you, the workshop simply would not have happened, and I feel like we've known each other much longer than we have.

Julia Borgini

My friend of more than 20 years and copy editor. Your attention to detail is something my brain is incapable of! You helped me learn how to translate my thoughts into words with clarity. And you helped a lot with spelling, grammer/sentence structure. See? ☺ Oh, and don't worry, the Habs will start their comeback tonight!

My QMO Team

Andrew Annett, Ardita Karaj, Bernadette Dario, and Bilal Iqbal for being the best team I've ever been a part of. We laughed, we cried, we almost got fired for going to a conference without telling our manager, but most of all, I learned a great deal from each of you, and would absolutely love to work with you all again in the future.

Sunish Chabba

Thank you for being one of my earliest supporters, and for designing the cover for the first edition of the book!

Neil LaChapelle

My structural editor! Thank you for helping take a dreadfully un-organized first edition book and helping me shape the new edition!

Muuks Creative
www.muuks.com

Kiitos! You did an amazing job on the images, layouts, and other material! I appreciate how you were able to create such simple, clean, and stunning images from complex ideas!

Gerry Weinberg, Esther Derby, Johanna Rothman, Don Gray, and Steve Smith

AYE 2009 was the trigger that changed how I think about change. Since then I've enjoyed numerous AYE conferences and PSL, and much of what I do today is inspired by what I experienced with you. Thank you for what you've given me over the years, and what you've given to the world of knowledge work.

CROWD-FUNDING BACKERS

Thank you to everyone who contributed to the crowd-funding campaign, without your support, no one would be reading this statement right now!

Pioneer Signature Backers

Gerald Chiva   Ivo van Halen

Pioneer Backers

Robie Wood	Jurgen Appelo	@Ferdinand
Robert Sundin	Lisette Sutherland	Sergey Kotlov
Jussi Höltta	Eric Siber	Alexandre Magno
Luis Gonçalves	Jaume Jornet	Ellen Gottesdiener
Geert De Cang	Thomas Baer	Andreas Wettstein

Early Adopters

Mark Levison	André Faria Gomes	Tomi Schuetz
Vasco Duarte	Sven Schnee	Henrique Imbertti Jr
Stefano Gatti	Fred Hoare	Pia-Maria Thoren
Chris Chapman	Tom Zigan	Jamie Longmuir
Nicolas Deverge	J. Barratt	Albrech Guenther

Early Access

Jussi Mäkelä	Flavius Stef	Martin Lennartz
Gerardo B. Palacios		

BETA READERS

Thank you to everyone who provided feedback during the pre-release
chapter phase, you helped me clarify ideas and fix typos!

Alicia Girard	Vijay Sai Reddy	Jonathan Harley
Craig Topper	Nadia Lamloum	Gregor Karlinger
Tobias Hilka	Peter Lam	Sunish Chabba
Joseph Soares	Neil LaChapelle	Clifford Sanders
Peter Trudelle	Wouter Zijlstra	Geoff Schaadt
Walmyr Lima	Silva Filho	Nancy Mazur
Travis Cord	Thawab Hazmi	Matthias Geiss
Paul Henman	Brad Booton	Celia Harquail
Ralph Hofman	Dirk Guldentops	Andrew Annett
Bernhard Fischer	David Dame	Daryl Conner
Melanie Frok	Dave Rooney	Michelle Berelowitz
Jorge Figueroa Arriagada		

Finally, thank you to anyone I missed! I've had so many conversations,
with so many people over the last couple of years I'm bound to have
left someone out!

REFERENCES

This is a combination of my bibliography and links to some of the tools, methods, and practices I referenced throughout the book.

Chapter 1
1 Virginia Satir Change Model – Steve Smith
   http://stevenmsmith.com/ar-satir-change-model/
2 Onirik Cracking the Change Code
   https://dl.dropboxusercontent.com/u/30239194/
   leanchangemanagement/cracking-the-change-code.pdf

Chapter 2
1 Behind Closed Doors – Johanna Rothman, Esther Derby
   http://pragprog.com/book/rdbcd/behind-closed-doors
2 PDCA Cycle – Walter Shewart
   https://www.deming.org/theman/theories/pdsacycle
3 Start Projects Red – Mike Edwards
   http://www.startred.com

Chapter 3
1 George Box
   http://en.wikiquote.org/wiki/George_E._P._Box
2 Prosci ADKAR®
   http://www.prosci.com/
3 Lean Coffee
   http://leancoffee.org/

Chapter 4
1 Information Radiators – Alistair Cockburn
   http://alistair.cockburn.us/Information%2Bradiator

2 Culture Hacking – Stephan Haas
http://bizculturehackers.com/

3 Agile Retrospectives – Esther Derby, Diana Larson
http://pragprog.com/book/dlret/agile-retrospectives

4 Force Field Analysis – Kurt Lewin
http://en.wikipedia.org/wiki/Force-field_analysis
http://www.mindtools.com/pages/article/newPPM_94.htm

5 OCAI Online
http://www.ocai-online.com/

6 Competing Values Framework
http://www.amazon.com/Diagnosing-Changing-Organizational-Culture-Competing/dp/0470650265

7 Becoming a Master Manager
http://www.amazon.com/Becoming-Master-Manager-Competing-Approach/dp/0470284668/

8 Managing Your Project Portfolio – Johanna Rothman
http://pragprog.com/book/jrport/manage-your-project-portfolio

9 The Re-Engineering Alternative – William Schneider
http://www.amazon.ca/The-Reengineering-Alternative-William-Schneider/dp/0071359818 (Sorry, can't find any online reference to William other than where to buy the book!)

Chapter 5

1 Kotter's 8-Step Change Model – John P. Kotter
http://www.kotterinternational.com

2 McKinsey 7S Framework
http://en.wikipedia.org/wiki/McKinsey_7S_Framework
http://www.tompeters.com/docs/Structure_Is_Not_Organization.pdf

3 Childers & Houston
http://www.researchgate.net/publication/239278291_Conditions_for_a_Picture-Superiority_Effect_on_Consumer_Memory/file/60b7d529ce9df9422a.pdf

4 Management 3.0 – Jurgen Appelo
http://www.management30.com

Chapter 6

1 Solution-focused Brief Therapy
http://en.wikipedia.org/wiki/Solution_focused_brief_therapy

2 Enclaria – Heather Stagl
http://www.enclaria.com

Chapter 7

1 Net Promotor Score
http://en.wikipedia.org/wiki/Net_Promoter

2 Toyota Kata – Mike Rother
http://www-personal.umich.edu/~mrother/Homepage.html

3 Are Happier Developers More Productive?
http://link.springer.com/chapter/10.1007%2F978-3-642-39259-7_7

Chapter 8

1 Neuralleadership – David Rock
http://www.scarf360.com/files/SCARF-NeuroleadershipArticle.pdf

2 Virtual Lean Coffee – Jason Little
http://www.agilecoach.ca/2014/02/15/running-100-virtual-lean-coffee/

3 Lean Change Management
http://www.leanchange.org

Author

1 4 Steps to an Agile Transformation
http://www.agilecoach.ca/2009/12/31/4-steps-to-an-agile-transformation/

2 A Guide to Organizational Change
http://www.agiletransformation.ca/

AUTHOR

AUTHOR

While working at a call centre that supported a global, enterprise organization in the late-90's, myself and a colleague decided to electronicize the paper-based operating and call routing tables. Why? Why not!

After seeing the 70 local and, who-knows-how-many, remote workers complain about how ineffective they were, we decided to learn how to program. A couple of weeks later, a Cold Fusion application running on Windows NT 3.51, O'Reilly's Website Pro with a Microsoft Access database was born!

That application seemed to make people happy, and it was possible because management let us do it, even though it wasn't part of our job description.

Over the years I moved away from development, and into project management and management. In 2007 I "officially" discovered

Agile and found my real passion. I say "officially" because what was known as "Agile" was just the way I preferred to work. What could be more awesome than inflicting Agile on organizations? How could they not love it!

After hitting many people over the head with the Agile stick for a couple of years I realized that implementing Agile had very little to do with Agile, and everything to do with change.

In 2009 I started experimenting with some ideas [1] that eventually morphed into a video series published by Pearson Education called Agile Transformation: A Guide to Organizational Change [2]. Here I debuted a one-page change plan, and began bridging the change management, organizational development and Agile communities.

In 2012 all the pieces fell into place. I had the opportunity to work with Jeff Anderson who was experimenting with applying Lean Startup concepts to implementing Kanban. Having recently launched two new products using the Lean Startup method, I was quite familiar with it already. Applying Lean Startup to change was the missing spice from my lean change management cookbook.

Later in 2012, I released the first edition of Lean Change Management and this second edition book is the next evolution of many innovative practices you can use to manage organizational change.

Made in the USA
Middletown, DE
30 September 2015